ASSASSINS' AMERICA

FOUR KILLERS, FOUR MURDERED PRESIDENTS, AND THE COUNTRY THEY LEFT BEHIND

BY JESSICA GUNDERSON & JOE TOUGAS

Capstone Young Readers
a capstone imprint

Assassins' America is published by Capstone Young Readers, a Capstone imprint
1710 Roe Crest Drive, North Mankato, Minnesota 56003
www.mycapstone.com

Library of Congress Control Number: 2017958324
ISBN 978-1-62370-981-5 (paperback)

Editorial Credits
Nick Healy, editor; Mackenzie Lopez and Kay Fraser, designers; Svetlana Zhurkin, media researcher; Tori Abraham, production specialist

Photo Credits
Bridgeman Images: Look and Learn/Rosenberg Collection, 7; Corbis Royalty-Free, 75; DVIC: NARA, 115, 117; Getty Images: Bettmann, 41, 83, 192, Corbis, 156, 158, De Agostini/A. Dagli Orti/DEA, 137, Fotosearch, 159, Hulton Archive, 78, 100, Kean Collection, 48, Leemage, 109, MPI, 16, Three Lions, 37, 169; John F. Kennedy Library and Museum, 153; LBJ Library Photo by Frank Muto, 154; Library of Congress, cover (right), 1, 2, 13, 14, 26, 28, 34, 38, 39, 40, 46, 53, 54, 58, 65, 68, 73, 77, 87, 88, 90, 95, 98, 102, 106, 110, 113, 123, 126, 132, 134, 136, 139, 141, 148, 163, 170, 180, 191; Newscom: Everett Collection, 164, 181, 187, 188, Mondadori Portfolio, 182, Picture History, 63, Universal Images Group/ Sovfoto, 166, Universal Images Group/Underwood Archives, 173, World History Archive, 10, Zuma Press/John F. Kennedy Library, 179, Zuma Press/Keystone Pictures USA, 151, Zuma Press/Keystone Press Agency, 146, Zuma Press/ Photoshot/Uppa, 185, Zuma Press/St. Petersburg Times/Tampa Bay Times, 176; North Wind Picture Archives, 118; Shutterstock: Everett Historical, cover (left, middle left, middle right), 5, 24, 31, 85, 120, 121; Svetlana Zhurkin, 19

Design Elements by Shutterstock

Printed and bound in China.
010736S18

TABLE OF CONTENTS

PART I. 1

President Lincoln's Killer and the America
He Left Behind

PART II. 47

President Garfield's Killer and the America
He Left Behind

PART III. .99

President McKinley's Killer and the America
He Left Behind

PART IV 147

President Kennedy's Killer and the America
He Left Behind

GLOSSARY. 196
SOURCE NOTES. 197
SELECT BIBLIOGRAPHY. 199
INDEX 201

INTRODUCTION

Abraham Lincoln died more than 150 years ago, but even now we live with the results of that shocking crime. The United States, historians agree, would be a different country today if Lincoln had lived.

President Lincoln had served barely 40 days of his second four-year term when he died. The Civil War had just ended. His work to heal the country and put it on a new path had barely begun. He would never get a chance to finish the job. Americans would never know what steps Lincoln might have taken to promote equality and freedom and to renew a country scarred by years of war.

President James Garfield was elected about 15 years after Lincoln died. Supporters expected Garfield to clean up government and to protect the rights of African Americans, who faced new forms of prejudice after the Civil War ended slavery in the United States. Garfield also would be denied a chance to finish his work. In fact, he'd barely begun. A deranged man shot Garfield just a few months into his presidency.

Twice more American presidents would die from assassins' bullets. Presidents William McKinley and John Kennedy were both popular leaders during times of change. They, too, would never have the chance to pursue their remaining goals as president. Each assassination would alter the country's path. Each death would have effects that would last long after the times in which the crimes took place.

Who were these assassins? A stage actor who was loyal to the South and angry over its defeat shot Abraham Lincoln. A troubled character who wanted a job in government shot James Garfield. A former factory worker who became fascinated with anarchists and their beliefs shot William McKinley. And a strange man who admired the communists leading Cuba and the Soviet Union shot John Kennedy. The stories of these crimes can be powerful and painful. They also raise many questions.

How would America be better off if none of its presidents had been assassinated? That's a difficult question to answer because, of course, we can never know for sure what each president might have accomplished — or failed to accomplish. We can, however, consider what these murdered leaders stood for, what they hoped and planned to do, and what might have happened if only they'd had the chance.

Abraham Lincoln

PART I

PRESIDENT LINCOLN'S KILLER AND THE AMERICA HE LEFT BEHIND

THE ASSASSIN, THE CRIME, AND ITS LASTING BLOW TO FREEDOM AND EQUALITY

John Wilkes Booth, an actor who became an assassin

CHAPTER 1
LINCOLN'S KILLER

Picture this: President Abraham Lincoln is about to speak from a balcony of the White House. For four long years, the North and South have clashed in bloody battles, leaving hundreds of thousands dead or wounded. But now peace has come at last. It's April 11, 1865. The Civil War is finally over.

Imagine yourself there in the crowd on the White House lawn. You're probably wearing heavy, scratchy clothes — a jacket and a high-buttoned collar, or a long, flouncy dress that's laced so tight it's hard to breathe. The sun has gone down, but the night air is stifling. Maybe you remove your hat and wipe your sweaty forehead, or perhaps you cool yourself with your fold-out fan.

And then you feel a chill at your back. Your whole body grows cold. You turn to find yourself face-to-face with John Wilkes Booth, the well-known stage actor. He's so famous you'd know him anywhere. All the girls your age adore him.

But something about him gives you the creeps. He wears an angry scowl on his face. His eyes smolder.

With a shudder, you return your attention to the White House balcony. The president has emerged and is talking about bringing the Union back together. "It is unsatisfactory that the black man is not allowed to vote," Lincoln says.

"Now, by God, I'll put him through!" hisses Booth. "That is the last speech he'll ever give."

Put him through? you think. *That means kill him. Did he really just say that?* You stare open-mouthed as Booth whirls around and stomps away.

You try to focus on the president and to hear his piercing voice, but you can't stop thinking about John Wilkes Booth, his murderous stare, and his threatening words. You should call for the police. But you can't, because this is long in the past, after all, and you aren't actually there.

A few days later, President Lincoln would be dead, and Booth — his assassin — would be on the run.

John Wilkes Booth was not what you might expect in a killer. He was handsome, charming, and famous. Think of your favorite movie star. *That's* about how famous he was. And he was young, only 26 years old. He had his whole life ahead of him. Then he made a decision that would change his life — and change the nation forever.

Booth — Johnnie, as many called him — grew up in Maryland, not terribly far from Washington, D.C. He came from a family of actors. His dad, Junius, was a famous actor who had made a name for himself performing Shakespeare's plays. Junius hailed from England and settled on a farm in Bel Air, Maryland, where John was born in

Junius Booth was a noted actor, and his sons followed in his footsteps.

1838. Maryland was a slaveholding state, and enslaved people tended the farm where he grew up.

Young Johnnie was theatrical from an early age. He loved to tromp through the woods near his home, giving speeches to an audience of trees and birds. He was often late for school. He sometimes got distracted by something on the walk there. He'd follow animals into the woods, making up stories about them. He was definitely more interested in what happened on the way to school than what happened in the classroom.

Booth's two older brothers were actors, like his father, and he wanted to follow in their footsteps. At age 17, John Wilkes Booth got his first chance on stage. He performed in one of Shakespeare's plays in Baltimore. His early performances showed such promise that he was invited to join a Shakespearean acting company. By age 22 he was making $20,000 a year as an actor. That's more than half a million dollars in today's money.

Booth gave bold and memorable performances on stage, and his good looks made him quite popular with the ladies. Often women would crowd around him as he left the theater, sometimes even ripping his clothes. Every day he received fan mail from women who adored him.

What could turn Booth, a beloved and admired actor, into a murderer? Was he A) a cold-blooded killer, B) a racist, C) out for revenge, or D) all of the above?

The answer is most likely D) all of the above. He had a variety of motives, but one thing is certain: He wasn't a madman acting in a moment of rage. His killing of Lincoln was carefully planned out. And he didn't do it alone. He had a web of accomplices.

★ ★ ★

What led to John Wilkes Booth wanting to kill the president in the first place? In 1860 Abraham Lincoln was elected president. Southern states feared Lincoln would make slavery illegal. Soon several Southern states decided to leave the Union and form their own country, the Confederate States of America. In April 1861 the Civil War between the Union and Confederacy broke out.

Maryland, Booth's home state, was a border state. Although it was a slave state, it did not join the Confederacy.

But Booth sided with the Confederacy. He was what was called a "Southern sympathizer" — someone who lived in the North but sided with the South. Booth believed that slavery was necessary and right. He also held staunchly racist views. He even wrote, "This country was formed for the white, not the black man."

But he didn't suit up in a Confederate uniform and join the fight. Instead he continued acting, mostly touring Northern cities. At times he spoke out passionately about preserving slavery, calling the South's secession heroic. He wrote: "I will not fight for secession . . . but I will fight heart and soul . . . for justice to the South." He hated President Lincoln and blamed him for the war. He called Lincoln a tyrant who wanted to destroy the South.

Booth and his co-conspirators first plotted to kidnap President Lincoln.

As the war went on and the dead piled up, Booth started to feel worthless. Thousands of young men his own age were dying or losing limbs for what they believed in. And all he was doing was acting and talking.

Desperate to do something — anything, it seemed — Booth began meeting with Confederate spies. He went to Montreal, Canada, where agents from the Confederate Secret Service, a network of spies, were meeting. As an actor he was able to cross borders without suspicion and travel through the North and the South. This would make it easy for him to smuggle information to Confederates. No one knows for sure if Booth actually became a spy, although he did claim to have smuggled medicine to the South.

By mid-1864 the war was turning sharply in the North's favor. Booth was enraged. He stopped acting altogether. He began meeting with Southern sympathizers at Mary Surratt's boardinghouse in Washington, D.C. He started plotting against the North and against President Lincoln.

★ ★ ★

On March 15, 1865, Booth sat in the back room of Gautier's Restaurant in the capital, gobbling oysters and downing champagne. In front of him was an audience of six men — George Atzerodt, David Herold, Lewis Powell, Samuel Arnold, Michael O'Laughlen, and John Surratt, a Confederate spy. He'd known some of them for years, others for mere months. But they all had one thing in common: They despised the North and Abraham Lincoln.

But this audience wasn't there to watch him act. They weren't even there to eat oysters and drink champagne. They were there to listen to Booth's plan.

Booth might've said something like this: *Listen, fellas. I heard that Lincoln will be attending a play at Campbell Hospital. We'll ambush him on his way home. Kill the driver, capture Lincoln, take him across the river to Virginia, Confederate territory. Then we'll put up a ransom. Lincoln in exchange for all Confederate prisoners.*

The plan seemed like it could work. Back then there was no Secret Service to protect the president. Lincoln usually traveled without guards. Booth and his conspirators figured they could easily overtake Lincoln's carriage. And if the ransom demand was met, Booth thought, the released prisoners would rejoin the Confederate Army. The South would regain military strength.

But Lincoln changed his mind and didn't go to Campbell Hospital. Surratt later said the group had approached a carriage in hopes of carrying out their plan two days after the restaurant meeting. The carriage held Secretary of the Treasury Salmon Chase, not Lincoln. Chase's carriage continued on, and Booth's plan failed.

But he was determined to try again. Three weeks later, on April 9, Confederate General Robert E. Lee surrendered to Union General Ulysses S. Grant. Although a few smaller armies still battled, the war was essentially over. The South had lost.

The South's surrender sent Booth into a rage. The Southern cause, which he'd become so passionate about, was now a lost cause. But maybe he could do something about it. Maybe the South could rise again.

All across Washington, D.C., crowds celebrated the end of the war. Booth didn't celebrate. He wandered the city in a dejected state. He clung to hope. Maybe the few remaining Confederate armies would refuse to surrender.

On April 11 Booth was in the crowd outside the White House as Lincoln spoke about the end of the war and giving freed slaves full citizenship. Booth made up his mind, right then and there, that Lincoln had to die. And he would be the one to kill him.

Abraham Lincoln as a young man

CHAPTER 2
LINCOLN'S STORY

Abraham Lincoln, the sixteenth president of the United States, is widely considered one of America's greatest presidents. He led the country through the Civil War with determination to keep the United States together and to defeat those who would break it apart. He declared that all slaves would be free, and with the war won, he spoke of binding up wounds. He was determined to repair the country and rebuild the South. He dreamed of brighter days until John Wilkes Booth shot him dead.

But long before all that, he was just a kid living a hardscrabble life in southern Indiana. He was born in 1809 in a one-room log cabin in Kentucky. Seven years later the Lincolns moved to Indiana, where Abe spent most of his childhood years. His life wasn't exactly easy. His mother died when he was nine. And he didn't get along with his father, Thomas. Abe liked to spend his time reading, and his dad thought he was lazy. Imagine! Calling Abe Lincoln — a kid who would eventually become president — lazy!

Abe had very little formal education. He liked school, but since the Lincolns were poor, he had to work to help support the family. He was mostly self-taught. He read anything he could find, often reading books over and over.

When Abe was 21, his family moved to Illinois. He joined them, although he didn't live with them for long. He worked a variety of jobs: boatman, storekeeper, militiaman, postmaster. He taught himself law and eventually became a lawyer. His law career led him on a path to the presidency.

Perhaps you've heard the story of "Honest Abe." The one where he walks 5 miles, uphill both ways, to return a nickel? Or was it 10 miles in a blizzard to return a library book? That story has many versions, but there is truth behind the legend. When he was working as a store clerk, Abe realized he hadn't given a customer the right amount of change. So he closed the store and walked several miles to return the correct change to the customer.

Honesty was only one of Lincoln's finer qualities. He was driven. He was intelligent. (Some historians think he was the smartest president in U.S. history.) He was charming and had a great sense of humor. He loved to tell jokes. His laughter helped lighten the mood and drew people to him.

But beneath the jokes, Lincoln struggled with depression and grief. Life had not been easy on his family. Long before Lincoln's presidency, his son Edward died at a young age in 1850. While in the White House, Lincoln's son Willie died in 1862 at age 11. The president had jarring mood swings. One minute he'd be laughing, and the next he'd be in despair. He called himself "the loneliest man in the world."

When Lincoln was running for president in 1860, the story of "Honest Abe" was used in campaign ads. Lincoln (Republican) ran against three top contenders: Stephen Douglas (Northern Democrat), John C. Breckinridge (Southern Democrat), and John Bell (Constitutional Unionist).

Abraham Lincoln frightened Southern slave owners. He was against the spread of slavery.

Willie Lincoln died of typhoid fever less than a year after his family moved into the White House.

In other words, he didn't want slavery to be legal in newly formed states and territories in the West. Southerners felt their way of life was under attack. So when Lincoln easily won the election, eight Southern states quickly seceded, or separated, from the United States to form their own country, the Confederate States of America. Four more states would eventually join them.

Lincoln wanted more than anything to keep the United States together. He felt secession was illegal according to the U.S. Constitution. Basically, he begged the South to come back. During his inauguration speech in March 1861, Lincoln stated that he would not interfere with slavery that already existed in the South, as long as the Confederate States rejoined the Union. But the Confederate leaders refused.

So Lincoln began his presidency with a country that was crumbling at his feet. Then Confederates fired on Union-held Fort

Sumter in Charleston, South Carolina. That was the first battle of the long, grisly Civil War, which killed more than 600,000 and left many Southern cities in ruins.

Lincoln is one of the most popular presidents today, but during his presidency, he was sharply criticized. He had many political enemies, some within his own party. Lincoln

Abraham Lincoln received about 40 percent of the popular vote and defeated three other candidates for the presidency in 1860.

had to make many tough decisions throughout the war, such as holding Confederate sympathizers in prison without trial. Many believed his actions went against Americans' rights and freedoms. But Lincoln believed these harsh actions were necessary in war times.

Lincoln is often called the Great Emancipator for his role in freeing slaves. But that wasn't always his goal. When he began his presidency, he wanted only to keep the Union together. He despised slavery, but he believed it was legal under the Constitution. He was willing to let the South hold on to slavery in order to save the nation.

Divided opinions over the future of slavery even reached into the president's family. Strange as it may seem now, Lincoln's wife came from a wealthy slaveholding family from Kentucky. Some of Mary Todd Lincoln's relatives even fought for the Confederacy.

By 1862, though, Lincoln's views on slavery had changed. He made up his mind to emancipate (or free) the slaves. With his famous Emancipation Proclamation on January 1, 1863, Lincoln declared slavery illegal in rebellious states. This raised the stakes for the Confederates: win the war or slavery dies. The proclamation also raised the stakes for Union troops. They were no longer fighting only to preserve the Union. They were fighting for human freedom. About the Emancipation Proclamation, Lincoln said, "If my name ever goes into history, it will be for this act."

By the war's end, Lincoln's views on slavery and African-American rights would move even further from where he stood before arriving in the White House. He would come to believe that African Americans should have equal rights.

As the war dragged on, Abraham Lincoln was haunted by all the death and destruction. He spent hours writing letters to dead soldiers' families, expressing his grief. The distress took a toll on his body. His face was now lined with wrinkles. The painter Francis Carpenter described him as having "great black rings under his eyes, such a picture of the effects of sorrow."

Despite his many critics and enemies, Lincoln never feared for his life. From his very first days in office, Lincoln began receiving death threats. He kept the most threatening letters in a cubbyhole of his desk. But he treated the threats lightly. He didn't think anyone would actually kill him. Even after a bullet whizzed by his head while he was riding a horse one summer night, he shrugged the threats off.

Lincoln was a great lover of theater and was also a fan of John Wilkes Booth. He saw Booth star in the play *The Marble Heart* in 1863. He sent invitations to Booth, asking him to visit the White House. But Booth never responded to the invitations. Little did Lincoln know that one day Booth would respond, and he would meet Lincoln's kindness with violence.

A depiction of the slaughter of anti-slavery settlers in Kansas

CHAPTER 3
TROUBLED TIMES

Years before Lincoln's election, an armed posse of 800 proslavery men descended upon Lawrence, Kansas. The date was May 21, 1856. The mob ransacked the newspaper offices, smashed the printing press, and burned papers and books. The men then ransacked and set fire to the town's hotel. As flames rose from the hotel, the mob marched through the streets, pillaging and burning all buildings that lay in their path. By nightfall the town was in smoldering ruins.

A few days later, the abolitionist John Brown and a group of his antislavery followers set out for revenge. They waited until night fell. Then they marched to the homes of five proslavery settlers, dragged them from their beds, and hacked them to death. This became known as the Pottawatomie Creek Massacre.

These skirmishes, along with others, caused the territory to become known as Bleeding Kansas. So what did Bleeding Kansas, far away on the western frontier, have to do with the Civil War? Bleeding Kansas was part of a fight over slave states and free states.

Tensions had been brewing for decades over the issue of free states, slave states, and whether slavery would grow into new territories. More and more people were settling the west. Settlers from the South brought their slaves with them. This led to a question: Should western territories and newly admitted states allow slavery?

After years of rising tension, a compromise was reached in Washington, D.C. The Compromise of 1850 stated, in short, that citizens of territories and states should decide for themselves whether slavery should be legal. The compromise brought a sense of relief to the American people. Many Americans feared that the slavery issue would break the nation apart, and the compromise seemed to calm these fears (or at least push the slavery issue aside).

The Kansas-Nebraska Act of 1854 echoed the Compromise of 1850. White settlers could choose by popular vote whether Kansas and Nebraska would be free or slave states. The territory of Kansas bordered Missouri, a slave state. Determined abolitionists poured into Kansas, hoping to make it a free state. Proslavery settlers also poured into the area, hoping to make it a slave state. Violence erupted as proslavery and antislavery factions attacked each other. From 1854 to 1861, 56 people died in Bleeding Kansas conflicts. Although the Civil War didn't officially begin until 1861, you could say Kansas saw the first blood spilled of the Civil War.

For many in the South, slavery was an important thread in the fabric of their lives. The first slaves were brought to American colonies in 1619, long before the United States became a nation. Slavery quickly spread throughout the colonies. More than 7 million slaves were brought from Africa in the 18th century. Slaves mostly worked on large farms and plantations along the Southern coast, toiling on tobacco, indigo, and rice plantations. In 1793 the invention of the cotton gin allowed for the growing of cotton in the South.

Slavery was not as widespread in the Northern states, and one by one Northern states moved to ban slavery within their borders. By 1804 slavery was illegal in all Northern states. In 1808 the United States outlawed

John Brown crusaded against slavery and used violence to advance his cause.

importing slaves from Africa. However, anyone born into slavery was a slave for life and could be bought or sold at any time.

The 1830s and 1840s saw the rise of the abolitionist movement — a movement to make slavery illegal in the United States. Abolitionists helped slaves escape through the Underground Railroad, a network of safe houses. Abolitionists also vowed to keep any new states from becoming slave states.

Those forces led to Bleeding Kansas and abolitionist John Brown. After the Pottawatomic Creek Massacre, Brown returned east and began thinking of a way to free slaves in Virginia. The best way to do it, he thought, was to arm slaves with weapons so they could rise up against their owners. In October 1859, Brown and 21 other men raided Harpers Ferry, an arsenal of federal weapons. They planned to steal weapons for the slave uprising, but their plan failed. John Brown was captured, put on trial, and sentenced to death for treason.

Before his hanging, Brown had to be heavily guarded in case he tried to escape. Volunteers lined up to guard him. Following along with some of those volunteers was the young actor John Wilkes Booth.

Booth both hated and admired John Brown. He didn't like what Brown stood for — the ending of slavery. But he admired that Brown had taken action for what he believed in. Some say Brown's hanging was the spark that led to John Wilkes Booth's assassination plan.

★ ★ ★

Where did Abraham Lincoln stand while all of this transpired? Lincoln was against the spread of slavery to new states and territories. As an individual, he believed slavery was wrong. But as a lawyer and politician, he believed that slavery was protected by the U.S. Constitution in the states where it already existed.

Even so, Lincoln's election in November 1860 was the final straw for many in the South. Lincoln hadn't carried a single Southern state. Southerners felt they were losing power in Washington, D.C. The loss of this power would mean that they couldn't carry out proslavery agendas. Seven states — South Carolina, Mississippi, Florida, Alabama, Georgia, Louisiana, and Texas — seceded from the Union. They established their own government under the Confederate States of America in February 1861, before Lincoln even officially took office. The Confederates chose Jefferson Davis to be their president.

The Confederacy seized Union forts throughout the South. But Union troops remained at Fort Sumter, in Charleston Harbor, South Carolina. On the morning of April 12, 1861, Confederate forces bombarded Fort Sumter. Eventually Union forces surrendered. The

Battle of Fort Sumter signaled the beginning of the Civil War. After Sumter, four more states — Arkansas, North Carolina, Tennessee, and Virginia — joined the Confederacy.

No one realized what a long and violent conflict awaited the country. Many people, including President Lincoln, thought the North would easily quash the South's rebellion. In July Union troops entered Virginia with the hopes of taking the Confederate capital of Richmond. It was a beautiful day, and many residents of Washington, D.C., decided to go watch the battle. They packed carriages with picnic lunches and set off to the battle site along the Bull Run River near Manassas Junction. Men and women perched atop a hill to watch the battle, almost as if they were attending a sporting event.

At first it seemed the Union would win. But the Confederates had amassed a large number of troops. A late afternoon Confederate charge sent the Union troops into a panicked retreat. Chaos erupted as troops and civilians scrambled away, back toward the capital.

With the First Battle of Bull Run, it was apparent that the war would not end quickly and would not be easily won. Confederate forces won significant victories in the first two years of the war. It seemed that the Union, which Lincoln had vowed to preserve, would fall.

The dead from both sides lay scattered across battlefields. The wounded filled hospitals. Prisoners of war filled Confederate and Union prisons. Disease and illness spread through army camps. As the war continued without an end in sight, many people — Northerners and Southerners alike — blamed President Lincoln.

Almost every family was affected by the war. Many men joined up or were drafted. Women were left to care for the family, often having to find jobs or tend farmland. Poor families were more affected by the war than the rich. In the North, men could avoid the draft by paying a $300 fee. In the South, men who owned at least 20 slaves didn't have to fight. In fact, many Confederate soldiers didn't even own slaves.

Most Civil War battles were fought in the South. Women and children witnessed war firsthand, right on their doorsteps.

It's important to note that not all Southerners supported the Confederacy. "Unionists" were people living in Confederate states who opposed secession. And not all Northerners wanted a war to preserve the Union. Anti-war Northerners were called "Copperheads." Southern sympathizers, like John Wilkes Booth, were those who lived in the North but supported the Southern cause. Also, not every slave state joined the Confederacy. The border states of Maryland, Delaware, West Virginia, Kentucky, and Missouri were slave states but remained in the Union.

On January 1, 1863, Lincoln took a stand against slavery with the Emancipation Proclamation. He announced that the goal of the war was not just to preserve the Union. Now the goal was also to eliminate slavery in the South.

Before the Emancipation Proclamation, free African Americans couldn't officially join the Union Army. But in the South, slaves were *forced* to support the war effort. They built forts and worked in armories and hospitals. The efforts of the slaves were helping the Confederacy — and continuing their enslavement.

After the Proclamation, African Americans could legally join the Union Army. Frederick Douglass, an abolitionist leader who'd escaped from slavery, urged his fellow African Americans to enlist.

Many of them did. About 190,000 African Americans fought for the Union by the end of the war.

In July 1863 a Union victory at the Battle of Gettysburg marked a major turning point in the war. Union victories now stacked up against Confederate victories. But Lincoln still faced scrutiny and opposition. In 1864 some Republican leaders believed Lincoln shouldn't even run for a second term. They felt he would surely lose to the Democratic candidate, General George B. McClellan. A faction of the Democratic Party wanted to negotiate for peace with the Confederacy, and whether or how McClellan might have continued the war was uncertain.

By September, though, the war looked like it was finally nearing the end. Union General William Tecumseh Sherman captured Atlanta, Georgia, in the heart of the South. It was a major victory. Lincoln won reelection.

With the end of war in sight, Lincoln was faced with the task of Reconstruction — rebuilding the nation and figuring out how to re-admit the Confederate states into the Union. Some members of his administration wanted the South to be punished harshly. Lincoln wanted mercy for the South. In his Second Inaugural Address, he said he wanted to rebuild the nation "with malice toward none, with charity for all."

But Abraham Lincoln was never able to put his plan for Reconstruction into effect. John Wilkes Booth would change the path of history with a single bullet.

Ford's Theatre in 1865

CHAPTER 4
BOOTH'S CRIME

John Wilkes Booth stopped by Ford's Theatre in Washington, D.C., on April 14, 1865. He was there to get his mail. But while there, he learned something that caused his pulse to quicken and his mind to race. That very night President Lincoln would be attending the play *Our American Cousin* at the theater. General Grant would be there with him.

What luck! This was Booth's chance. He knew the theater inside and out. He'd performed there many times. He knew exactly where the president would be sitting — the Presidential Box in the balcony. He knew the play line by line too. While the audience was laughing uproariously at a funny line, Booth could creep into the Presidential Box, kill the president and General Grant, and escape amidst the chaos.

But his idea went even further. What if he took out not only Lincoln and Grant, but also Vice President Andrew Johnson and Secretary of State William Seward? With its top leaders dead,

Lincoln and his cabinet, which included others whom Booth plotted to kill

the government would collapse. The Union would collapse, he imagined. The South could rise again!

And Booth had a team of conspirators to help him carry out the plan.

Booth scurried from the theater. He had a lot to do to put his plan in place. First he went to a livery stable and secured a getaway horse. Booth knew he would need to escape Washington after the assassination. He would head south. Once he crossed into Virginia, a Confederate state, he'd be safe, he figured.

He visited his friend Mary Surratt and told her to have weapons ready at her tavern along their escape route. (No one knows if he told her of the assassination plot. Remember that. It will be important later.)

Booth headed to a tavern and had a drink. Then he wrote a letter to a newspaper, the *National Intelligencer*. In the letter, he described that his plans had changed from kidnapping to assassinating Lincoln. He signed his name along with the names of David Herold, Lewis Powell, and George Atzerodt. He gave the letter to a friend, John Mathews, and told him to deliver it the next day.

Why on earth would Booth send a letter to a newspaper confessing his crime? And before it even happened? Here's why: Booth was proud of his plan. He thought others would be proud of him too. He thought he would be revered. He figured he'd be a hero for saving the nation from the "tyrant" Abraham Lincoln. That's not quite what happened.

While Booth was giving his letter to Mathews, he glimpsed a carriage passing by. Inside was General Grant. The carriage was headed toward the train station. He realized Grant was not going to be attending the theater that night. But he was still determined to kill Lincoln.

Booth went back to Ford's to make some final preparations. The Presidential Box was a private balcony seat that had two doors, an outer door and an inner door. Booth may have carved a hole in the frame of the outer door — or perhaps the hole was already there. Either way, he planned to wedge in a wooden stick, barring the door from the inside. After slipping into the box, he would put the makeshift lock in place. Anyone who suspected that something was wrong would have to break down the door. By then, Booth figured, the deed would be done.

At points throughout the day, Booth met with his accomplices — Lewis Powell, David Herold, and George Atzerodt. Who were these guys, and what tasks did Booth give them?

Lewis Powell (alias Lewis Payne) was a Confederate soldier who'd been wounded and captured at the Battle of Gettysburg. He escaped a Union hospital and went on to serve in a Confederate cavalry unit called Mosby's Regiment. He left the unit and took an oath of allegiance to the Union. He likely took this oath so he could be a Confederate spy. Booth told him to go to Secretary Seward's house that evening at 10:15 p.m. Seward was recovering from a carriage accident, so would be in his bed. Powell was told to pretend he was there to deliver medicine — and to kill Seward once inside.

David Herold was an avid hunter and pharmacist's assistant. His knowledge of backwoods would make him helpful in the assassins' getaway from the capital. Booth gave him an assignment. He was to wait for Powell outside Seward's house. Together they were to leave the city and meet the rest of the group at Soper's Hill, Maryland.

George Atzerodt was a German immigrant who owned a carriage repair business in Maryland. At Booth's order, he was

David Herold

staying at the Kirkwood House in Washington, D.C. This is where Vice President Johnson was also staying. Booth told Atzerodt to go to Johnson's room around 10 o'clock that night — and to kill him.

The accomplices had one final meeting that evening. The stage was set. Each accomplice knew his role. By the end of the night, the top leaders of the

U.S. government would be dead. If all went according to plan, that is.

Meanwhile, Abraham Lincoln woke that morning having no inkling that day would be his last. He was in jolly spirits. The war was over. A new dawn was breaking for the United States. And he, Lincoln, would lead the country from darkness to light.

Lincoln met with his cabinet that morning. He told his advisers that he hoped to be lenient with the South. Secretary of War Edwin Stanton disagreed. He thought the South should be punished. General Grant was also at the meeting. He told Lincoln he wouldn't be able to go to the play with him that night. Mary Lincoln invited Major Henry Rathbone and his fiancée, Clara Harris, instead.

In the afternoon Lincoln and his wife took a carriage ride. Mary complained of a headache and told her husband they should stay home that night. But Lincoln insisted on going to Ford's Theatre.

Around 8 p.m. the President and First Lady set off for the theater, picking up Henry Rathbone and Clara Harris on the way. They were late. The play was already in progress. When the group stepped into the theater, the actress on stage spotted Lincoln. She stopped performing and began clapping. Soon the entire crowd was giving Lincoln a standing ovation as he took his seat in the Presidential Box.

The play resumed, and Lincoln grabbed his wife's hand. After four long years of war, he was feeling at peace.

★ ★ ★

Just after 9:30 p.m., Booth galloped on his rented horse to the alley behind Ford's Theatre. He leapt off the horse and threw the reins to a theater worker. "Hold my horse for a bit," he told the worker. "I'll be back." Then he slipped in the back door and listened.

The play had begun. He knew the play well, and he knew it would be another hour until the actor Harry Hawk spoke the humorous line that would make the audience erupt in laughter, drowning out the gunshot.

He crept beneath the stage and went out the side door. He could use a drink to calm his nerves. He headed next door to Taltavul's Saloon and ordered whiskey. The clock was ticking. It was almost time.

Booth strode through the front door of the theater, greeted the ticket clerk, and made his way upstairs to the balcony. A few theater-goers recognized him, whispering as he passed. He paid his fans no attention. He was on a mission.

Only one man — the President's footman Charles Forbes — stood outside the door to the Presidential Box. Booth showed him his calling card. Forbes nodded and let him in.

Quickly and quietly Booth slid the stick of wood into place to bar the door. He could hear the actors' lines from the stage. Quietly he opened the second door. Then he heard his cue: "Don't know the manners of good society, eh? Well, I guess I know enough to turn you inside out, old gal; you sockdologizing old man-trap!"

The audience exploded with laughter. Booth's gun exploded too. A single shot slammed into the back of Lincoln's head.

The gunshot echoed throughout the theater. Gun smoke drifted into the air. Major Rathbone leapt from his seat and tried to tackle Booth. In the scuffle the gun clattered to the floor. But Booth had another weapon — his knife. He slashed Rathbone in the arm. Rathbone staggered back. Blood from his wound sprayed the box.

Booth shouted grandly as he jumped to the stage below.

Lincoln, his wife, and their guests had turned their attention to the stage when Booth entered the Presidential Box. They didn't notice him until he fired his pistol.

He said, "Sic Semper Tyrannis!" — meaning "Thus always to tyrants!" His left ankle snagged on one of the banners on the balcony, and he fell awkwardly. The crowd buzzed with confusion. What was the famous John Wilkes Booth doing on stage? Was this part of the play? Why was Mary Lincoln screaming, "Stop that man!"?

Before anyone could realize President Lincoln had just been shot, Booth scurried, limping, out the back door and hurdled onto his horse. Then he raced away into the night.

★ ★ ★

Around the same time, Lewis Powell and David Herold approached Secretary Seward's home, according to most histories of the evening. Powell banged on the door while Herold waited in the shadows. "I'm here to deliver medicine to the secretary," Powell told the servant who opened the door. When the servant refused to let him in, Powell pushed his way through the door and ran up the stairs. Two of Seward's sons tried to stop him, but Powell bludgeoned one son with his gun and stabbed the other with his dagger.

He then burst through Secretary Seward's door, pounced upon him, and stabbed him three times. Seward's nurse tried to pull Powell off, but he stabbed the nurse too. Then Powell ran down the stairs, slashing two more who tried to stop him. He dashed out into the night, leaving the bloody scene behind, ready to climb on the horse and take off out of town. But the horse was not there — nor was David Herold.

Herold, spooked by the screams coming from inside the house, had galloped away, leaving Powell behind.

Powell wandered and hid himself in the city for days. All roads out of Washington, D.C., were blocked. He was stuck there with no hope of reconnecting with Booth and the others.

★ ★ ★

And what of George Atzerodt's attempts to kill Vice President Johnson? Before the planned time of assassination, Atzerodt was beginning to get cold feet. He went to a bar to get a drink. But he didn't stop at just one drink. He drank and drank. Maybe he forgot what he was supposed to do. Or maybe he lost his courage. Or perhaps he was too drunk to do it. In any case, he went back to his room and fell asleep. He made no attempt whatsoever to kill Johnson. Atzerodt would say later that he had been part of the failed kidnapping plan but had never agreed to assassinate Johnson.

★ ★ ★

Back at Ford's Theatre, Dr. Charles Leale was the first to come to Lincoln's aid. The president was still breathing. His head was cradled in his wife's lap as she hunched over him, weeping. Dr. Leale examined him, finding that the bullet was lodged in the president's skull. There was no saving him. Leale then uttered the dreaded words: "His wound is mortal."

Lincoln was carried across the street to the Petersen Boarding House, where he could die in peace. A sobbing Mary and several solemn cabinet members and doctors surrounded him, watching him struggle to live. At 7:22 the next morning, President Abraham Lincoln breathed his last.

And his killer, John Wilkes Booth, was still on the loose.

Rewards were offered for Booth and his accomplices when they were

CHAPTER 5
THE AFTERMATH

Panic gripped Washington, D.C. President Lincoln was dead. Secretary of State William Seward had narrowly survived a gruesome attack. Clearly, a conspiracy was afoot. Who was next?

Members of Congress and Lincoln's cabinet huddled at their homes, afraid to leave. What if they were targets? No one knew how far the conspiracy spread. And no one knew who was behind the conspiracy. People wondered if the Confederates had plotted with Booth to kill Lincoln. They wondered if war would begin again.

In the days following the assassination, angry mobs stormed prisons holding Confederate soldiers. Any man who looked even a little bit like Booth was apprehended and questioned. Southern sympathizers were attacked. Some historians believe that nearly 200 Southern sympathizers were killed to avenge Lincoln's death.

But along with the rage came a deep sorrow. Black flags draped homes and businesses. Any parades or parties celebrating the end of the war were canceled.

African Americans feared that the death of Lincoln meant the death of the Emancipation Proclamation. Many wondered whether they'd be thrown back into slavery.

Not everyone mourned Lincoln, though. Some newspapers in the South celebrated his death. Some Northerners did too. They blamed him for the war that had wrecked their country. But many people on both sides grieved and worried. No one knew how the nation would fare without Lincoln at the helm.

The night of the assassination, Secretary of War Edwin Stanton organized a manhunt to catch John Wilkes Booth and his accomplices. Booth's room was raided. One by one, suspects were rounded up. On April 17 Lewis Powell, after days of wandering around and sleeping in a cemetery, was arrested when he found his way to Mary Surratt's boardinghouse. Mary Surratt, Michael O'Laughlen, Samuel Arnold, and Ned Spangler (a stagehand at Ford's Theatre) were also arrested. A few days later, authorities found George Atzerodt hiding at his cousin's house. Dr. Samuel Mudd was arrested after housing Booth and David Herold for a night.

But John Wilkes Booth was still nowhere to be found. A massive search effort covered the countryside, from Washington, D.C., to Virginia, the largest manhunt the nation had ever known. Search parties fed off tips and often narrowly missed Booth and Herold.

After the assassination Booth and Herold met up at Soper's Hill. When Powell and Atzerodt didn't show, they continued on. For 12 days, Booth and Herold stayed on the run, hiding in the woods, making their way across swampland, engaging the help of known Confederates, and wearing disguises and pretending to be soldiers returning from the war. All the while Booth read reports of his deed.

John Wilkes Booth's final hiding spot was in a barn in Virginia, where troops set the building ablaze, shot Booth, and dragged him out.

Expecting to be hailed a hero, he was dismayed at being called a coward by the newspapers. Afraid, cold, hungry, and dirty, he railed against his fate: "I struck boldly and not as the papers say," he wrote in his diary. "Our country owed all her troubles to him . . . After being hunted like a dog . . . I am here in despair."

On April 26 Booth and Herold were staying in the Garrett family barn in Virginia. In the wee morning hours, federal authorities surrounded the barn, demanding Booth emerge. He refused. So the authorities set fire to the barn, hoping to flush them out. Herold surrendered, but Booth still refused. He swung open the barn door and, silhouetted by flames, raised his gun. Fearing Booth would fire, a young soldier named Boston Corbett shot him. Booth collapsed

The scene moments before several of Booth's accomplices where hanged for their crimes

and was dragged out. He died soon thereafter, murmuring, "Tell Mother I die for my country."

The other conspirators were put on trial. George Atzerodt, Lewis Powell, David Herold, and Mary Surratt were sentenced to death. But wait . . . why was Mary Surratt sentenced to die? Did she really have much to do with the assassination? Did she even know about the assassination plot? Historians are unsure of the extent of her role and her knowledge of events. In court prosecutors maintained that her boardinghouse was the nest where the plot was hatched. Mary claimed she had nothing to do with the assassination and that she was innocent. But still, she was hanged along with the others. Mary Surratt was the very first woman to be executed by the U.S. government.

After his death Lincoln's body was placed on a funeral train to carry him from Washington, D.C., to his final resting place of Springfield, Illinois. The train retraced the route Lincoln had traveled back in 1861 to take office, a distance of 1,654 miles. Mourners lined the tracks to bid goodbye to the president. The funeral procession made several stops in various cities. In New York City, thousands gathered as the horse-drawn hearse moved through the streets. From a high window, a little boy leaned out to watch the funeral procession. The boy was Theodore "Teddy" Roosevelt. Years later Teddy would become president after the assassination of President William McKinley.

Thanks perhaps to George Atzerodt's drunken cowardice, Vice President Andrew Johnson was very much alive and able to take on the role of president. But Johnson had none of Lincoln's political knowledge and skill. And worse, he didn't believe in equal rights for African Americans.

In the years following Lincoln's death, the nation set about reconstructing the South and re-admitting Confederate states into the Union. Johnson took control of Reconstruction, and historians far and wide believe he botched it.

At first Radical Republicans thought Johnson would be tough

The train carrying President Lincoln's casket drew large crowds as it traveled from Washington, D.C., to Illinois.

on the South. Secretary of War Edwin Stanton wanted Confederate leaders punished. But instead, Johnson wanted to deal with them lightly. Johnson himself was a Southerner, hailing from North Carolina and Tennessee. He came from a background of poverty, and he felt resentment against wealthy white planters in the South. So, rather than holding all Southern whites accountable for secession, he pardoned all whites except for wealthy planters and Confederate leaders. With this pardon, whites regained their property and political rights.

Consider this for a moment: white Southerners regaining their land. How did this affect the newly freed slaves? Some Republican leaders felt the slaves should be given land as reparation — in other words, as compensation for the hardship of slavery. Republican leaders thought slaves should be given the land they had worked on. But when Johnson gave the land back to previous white owners instead, many newly freed slaves had no choice but to work for white landowners. Most African Americans had no other way to make a

President Andrew Johnson

living. In effect this led to a system of white landownership and black servitude, a system that was hardly different from slavery.

Stanton and other Radical Republicans also wanted the federal government to have a strong presence in the South. But Johnson felt otherwise. He permitted states to form their own local governments, allowing them

40

to eventually create their own laws. This led to "black codes." Black codes took away civil liberties for African Americans in the South. These laws restricted the rights of African Americans to vote, own property, and own guns. Black codes also punished any African Americans who were out of work, making them criminals. For the next 100 years, African Americans in the South would not have the same legal rights as whites. African Americans had to go to different schools, eat at different restaurants, and drink from different water fountains. During Reconstruction the Ku Klux Klan emerged as a hate group that launched violent acts against African Americans and other groups. Racism remained strong in the South, stoked by Johnson's failed Reconstruction policies.

In the 1950s African Americans rose up against segregation in the Civil Rights Movement. You may have heard of Rosa Parks. In 1955 Parks refused to give up her seat to a white man in Montgomery, Alabama. This led to a city-wide bus boycott. Leading the boycott was a young minister named Dr. Martin Luther King Jr. He went on to become the most famous and inspiring leader of the Civil Rights Movement.

Rosa Parks refused to give up her seat on a city bus in Montgomery, Alabama.

At long last the Civil Rights Movement resulted in changed laws for African Americans in the South. A different President Johnson — Lyndon B. Johnson — signed the Civil Rights Act of 1964 and the Voting Rights Act of 1965. (Coincidentally,

President Lyndon B. Johnson became president after a presidential assassination too — the assassination of John F. Kennedy.) These acts protected equal rights for African Americans.

So, what might have happened if John Wilkes Booth hadn't gone to Ford's Theatre that fateful morning to pick up his mail? Or if his bullet missed its mark? What would Reconstruction have been like under President Lincoln? Would we even know the names of Martin Luther King Jr. or Rosa Parks? If Lincoln had lived, would racial segregation in the South have existed for so long? Would we, perhaps, have had an African-American president long before Barack Obama?

No one knows the answer to these questions, but many historians have speculated what America would have been like if Lincoln lived.

Lincoln didn't live long enough to create a solid plan for Reconstruction, but he definitely had some ideas in mind. He wanted equal citizenship and voting rights for African Americans. He wanted a "practical system by which the two races could gradually live themselves out of their old relation to each other, and both come out better prepared for the new."

In other words, he wanted a system that would help blacks and whites overcome racism and resentment. One way to secure voting rights for freed slaves was to allow Confederate states back into the Union only if they allowed African Americans to vote.

Another of Lincoln's plans was to divide land that had been abandoned or seized into 40-acre plots. Former slaves would be given these plots to farm, and, after three years, they could buy the land. This would allow them to make a living for themselves. If this had happened, many newly freed slaves wouldn't have had to work for white landowners and remain in poverty.

And what of Confederate leaders? Lincoln didn't want to punish Confederate leaders, but he did want to "scare them off." He hoped that if Confederate leaders left the country, new leaders — both black and white — would emerge in the South. Instead, many Confederate leaders remained in power.

Perhaps most importantly, some historians believe Lincoln would have been able to work with Radical Republicans such as Edwin Stanton to form a strong and lasting plan for the South. Instead, President Johnson and the Radical Republicans never agreed. The constant bickering between Johnson and Stanton led to Johnson firing Stanton. In retaliation, the Radical Republicans brought charges against Johnson to remove him from office. After a trial, Johnson was acquitted by only one vote, and he remained president. All of this was a distraction from what was really important: rebuilding the South and securing equal rights for African Americans.

Other historians believe, however, that the nation wouldn't have been any better off if Lincoln had lived. He might not have been able to overcome resistance to his ideas. His plans for Reconstruction might not have been able to happen without placing a large military force in the South. And voters might have opposed funding such a huge military expense. Additionally, Lincoln would have been in office until only 1869. That wouldn't have given him much time to put his policies into place.

What do you think might have happened if Lincoln lived? Would the nation be in a better place today? We will never know. But one thing is certain: A single man, a single bullet, and a single second changed the course of history.

TIMELINE >>>>>>>>>>>>>>>>>>>>>>>>

Feb. 12, 1809: Abraham Lincoln is born in Kentucky

1830: The Lincoln family moves to Illinois

1834: Lincoln is elected to Illinois state legislature

1836: Lincoln receives his law license

May 10, 1838: John Wilkes Booth is born near Bel Air, Maryland

1842: Lincoln marries Mary Todd

1846: Lincoln is elected to U.S. House of Representatives

1855: Booth makes his first stage appearance as an actor in Shakespeare's *Richard III*

1859: Booth witnesses the execution of abolitionist John Brown

1860: Lincoln is elected president of the United States

1861: The Civil War begins at Fort Sumter, South Carolina

1862: The Lincolns' son Willie dies from typhoid

1863: Lincoln watches Booth perform in the play *The Marble Heart*

1863: The Emancipation Proclamation is issued

1864: Booth begins forming a plot to kidnap President Lincoln

March 1865: Booth's plan to kidnap President Lincoln fails

April 9, 1865: Confederate General Robert E. Lee surrenders to Union General Ulysses S. Grant

April 14, 1865: Booth shoots Lincoln at Ford's Theatre

April 15, 1865: Lincoln dies of his wounds; Andrew Johnson is sworn in as president

April 26, 1865: Booth is shot and killed by Sergeant Boston Corbett in Virginia

March 27, 1866: Johnson vetoes the Civil Rights Act, which protected rights of African Americans; Congress overrides his veto

Feb. 24, 1868: President Johnson is put on trial after firing Secretary of War Edwin P. Stanton

May 26, 1868: The Senate finds Johnson not guilty

1870: All former Confederate States have been readmitted into the Union

1876: Reconstruction officially ends

1964–65: The Civil Rights Act and Voting Rights Act finally give legal equality to African Americans

James Garfield

PART II

PRESIDENT GARFIELD'S KILLER
AND THE AMERICA HE LEFT BEHIND
THE ASSASSIN, THE CRIME,
THE HAPLESS DOCTORS, AND
A PRESIDENT'S SLOW, GRIM DEATH

James Garfield at age 14

CHAPTER 6
AN UNLIKELY PRESIDENT

Imagine you've been assigned to write a long research paper on any U.S. president. It's due soon. Like tomorrow. And for the fun of it, let's also say you haven't done a thing yet. Suddenly, you need to think and work fast, and the first move is choosing your subject.

George Washington? Abraham Lincoln? Thomas Jefferson? Extraordinary leaders, all of them. They lived amazing lives in momentous times, achieving a greatness that forever shaped the United States. Such greatness will also keep you up all night researching and writing.

No, you need to pick a president who didn't change our world all that much, somebody to whom history books devote small, handy chapters. This may lead you to President James Garfield, who was in office for only a few short months before he was shot.

You may already see your report taking shape: elected, shot, died, and done. Simple, right? Maybe. But be warned: You may accidentally find yourself drawn in when you learn about James

Garfield. And you may find yourself sorry that he wasn't president for longer, because Garfield might have been a great president — another one of those people remembered for shaping his country.

Garfield was an early believer in civil rights, and with former slaves being brutalized by whites in the South, civil rights needed believers, especially at the presidential level. He also pledged to take a firm stand against government officials who took part in crooked, unfair practices that rewarded favors instead of honest work for the American people. He gave hope to working families across the country because he knew what it was like to grow up poor and how miserable it could be.

Garfield seemed ready to fight for the kind of changes that were overdue in the United States. The Civil War had ended about 15 years earlier, but the country was not making good on its promises of freedom and equality for all. Former slaves found their freedoms limited in new ways. Racial prejudice prevailed in many places and ways. Because he was gunned down four months after taking office, Garfield was unable to finish — or even really begin — what he wanted to accomplish.

Born in Ohio, Garfield was the kind of person others talk about when they mention America as a land of opportunity, a country where people can succeed no matter where they begin. As a boy, Garfield's life was marred by sadness and extreme poverty. As a man, he was a leader who, in a desire to help his fellow Americans, rose to the office of president of the United States.

Garfield's father moved to Ohio from New York in the early 1800s, first helping build the Ohio and Erie Canal, then making a go as a farmer. He married Eliza Ballou, and the couple farmed in the Ohio countryside. Sadly, James, born November 19, 1831, never knew his father, who died when the future president was 1 year old.

Following her husband's death, Eliza Garfield worked hard to not only put food on the table but to keep her four kids at home. In those days poverty often tore families apart, and the Garfields were indeed poor. James didn't get a pair of shoes until he was 4 years old. The home his family shared was a one-room log cabin with three small windows, the panes of which were oiled paper.

In such situations, the people often sent their children away to better-off homes with hope of giving them a comfortable life. Although Eliza was encouraged to do this, she kept her children. She tried to make the best of their poor conditions. She knew that education held James' key to escaping a future of poverty, but his interests were more in the working life, like his father.

Eager to work on the water, James at age 16 took work as a canal man on the Erie and Ohio Canal. His time in that job proved to be dangerous. Unable to swim, he nearly drowned after falling off the boat one evening, and shortly afterward, he contracted malaria. The disease, which is caused by a parasite infecting the blood, killed many of its victims. With her son at risk of an early death, James' mother offered him the grand total of $17 in hopes he would use it to go back to school.

Believing that his life was spared for a reason, James agreed to start attending school. From local schools he went to northern Ohio, where he enrolled in a small prep school called Western Reserve Eclectic Institute. He earned his tuition by working as a janitor for the school. James took to his subjects with great passion and fascination.

His school work was so successful that the school promoted him from janitor to professor. While in his second year of studies, James also began teaching classes including literature, math, and ancient languages.

In 1854 he was accepted to Williams College in Williamstown, Massachusetts, opening the world to him even further. He graduated with honors and returned to Ohio to teach at the Western Reserve Eclectic Institute. He became the school's president at age 26.

In 1858 Garfield married a former student of his from Western Reserve Eclectic Institute, Lucretia Rudolph. After Lucretia graduated, she and Garfield had exchanged letters, growing quite fond of each other. They would go on to have two daughters and five sons.

Garfield entered the world of politics in 1859 when a state senator died. Garfield was encouraged to run in an upcoming election, and he did so successfully. The Civil War soon interrupted his political career. He had hardly settled into office when the war broke out.

Eager to join the Union Army, he was made lieutenant colonel and showed himself to be a smart military thinker and strategist. In the Battle of Middle Creek, he fooled the Confederates into thinking his regiment was larger than it was. In attacking the much larger Confederate regiment from three sides, the appearance was enough to send the Confederates retreating and out of Kentucky. The battle made him famous. He was made a general, and ten months later in 1862, he was elected to the U.S. Congress.

In Congress, Garfield believed part of his role was to help the people like those he lived with as child, studied with as a student, and fought with as a soldier. He helped create jobs in the areas of westward expansion — the development of roads, businesses,

Mollie, Harry, James, Irving, and Abe Garfield (from left) were five of James and Lucretia Garfield's seven children.

Garfield rose to the rank of major general during the Civil War.

and communities in western states. He was particularly passionate about civil rights for African Americans. To that end, he introduced a measure that allowed black people to walk freely in Washington, D.C., without a pass. Today it may boggle the mind to think such a law would be necessary. In Garfield's time, racial prejudice had powerful friends in politics. Garfield and others fought for small victories for fairness and equality.

As a congressman, Garfield gave an acclaimed speech in support of allowing African Americans the right to vote when the war ended. He proved to be a strong ally of President Abraham Lincoln. Garfield won reelection overwhelmingly in 1864.

Sixteen years later, with the Civil War long over, President Lincoln's assassination remained a wound the nation hadn't healed. In 1880 the Republicans sent delegates to Chicago to choose their next nominee for president. By then Lincoln's party was divided into two groups, known as the Stalwarts and the Half-Breeds. The Stalwart Republicans — led by Senator Roscoe Conkling of New York, were those who enjoyed and benefitted from the spoils system. Under the spoils system, politicians gave powerful jobs as rewards to friends for their votes, money, or other forms of loyalty.

Conkling owed his wealth and power to the spoils system. He oversaw The New York Customs House, which handled most of the money that came in from taxing imports. He gave jobs — often with very good pay — to his political friends, and he steered government policy to reward the people and business that supported him. With such power, Conkling could control many politicians. Those who opposed his wishes could find themselves without a job. Conkling wanted to make sure the spoils system remained in place.

★ ★ ★

The Republican Party's convention in 1880 took place in Chicago, and it was a long, complicated, and testy affair. The party had a sitting president in the White House, but Rutherford B. Hayes had decided not to seek a second term. At the convention, Conkling and the Stalwarts aimed to nominate Ulysses S. Grant. The heroic general from the Civil War had already served two terms as president, from 1869 to 1877. The Stalwarts wanted to send him back for a third term, something no president had ever done.

The Half-Breed group, however, aimed to make James G. Blaine the party's candidate. Blaine was a senator from Maine, and he had previously served in the U.S. House of Representatives. He was also engaged in a political feud with Conkling and his allies. A third candidate, John Sherman of Ohio, also vied for delegates at the convention. Sherman was a former senator from Garfield's home state of Ohio, and Sherman was Secretary of the Treasury under Hayes. Sherman made a difficult candidate, though. His personality was so calm and reserved that he'd been nicknamed the Ohio Icicle.

As a delegate in Chicago, Conkling gave a speech to support Ulysses S. Grant, considered the favorite to be nominated as the Republican choice for president. On the first ballot, Grant got 304 votes, while Blaine had 285 and Sherman a mere 93. To get the nomination, a candidate would need 379 votes. Speeches were made, and more votes were taken. Through more than 30 ballots, no man reached the total required to be the party's nominee.

Garfield was well known as a good senator, a gifted writer, and a dynamic speaker. At the convention, his speech given in support of fellow Ohioan John Sherman proved this. The speech drew thunderous applause, and Garfield himself drew attention from many of the delegates.

Eventually his name was submitted at the convention as a possible Republican candidate for the presidency. He wasn't interested in the job and likely didn't think his name would rise in the convention voting. But he was wrong. Party delegates voted again and again. Grant never mustered enough support to claim the nomination. Two days and more voting later, the nomination went to the one man who wanted it least: James Garfield.

He was less than thrilled. Having seen good men run ragged in their desire to be president, Garfield had no personal interest in the job. But he also believed he could make a difference — perhaps where previous presidents could not. He believed this was his purpose. Shortly after receiving and accepting the nomination, he told a well-wisher, "I am very sorry that this has become necessary."

As the nominee, he faced off against Democrat Winfield Scott Hancock, a Civil War hero who had no experience in public office. The election was too close to call on election day itself, and Garfield went to bed before the votes were tallied. He woke up to the news that he was elected president. Garfield began making plans to move with his family, including his mother (a very proud Eliza Garfield) to Washington, D.C.

Mere months later in that city he would be shot at a train station. He would die not only from the wound, but from the shoddy medical care he received.

Charles J. Guiteau

CHAPTER 7
GARFIELD'S KILLER

Both James Garfield and his killer, Charles Guiteau, believed they were put on Earth to do something special. Garfield thought his purpose was to make people's lives better. And after a life that included being a teacher and war hero, becoming president was his biggest opportunity yet to do just that. At that same time, Guiteau would begin telling people he believed that he was put on Earth to kill President Garfield.

Looking at the lives of these two men, opposite tales emerge. With each chance Garfield took and with each new adventure — whether attending college, leading soldiers, or running for political office — he was a winner. Charles Guiteau, just as ambitious, seemed to meet failure at every turn. As Garfield's successes mounted, the life of Charles Guiteau seemed to collapse. He finally snapped, sending him toward one violent act that resulted in Garfield's death and, eventually, in Guiteau's own death.

It's a tragic story, the life of Charles Guiteau. Up until his murderous act, you could almost feel sorry for him. In fact, in today's world, he would be likely recognized as having serious mental illness and needing treatment and therapy. And although there were homes and treatments for obviously insane people, as he might have been called in his day, he never received any such help.

Guiteau's childhood began on an Illinois farm where, after losing his mother when he was 7, he was raised by his father, Luther Guiteau. (Their last name is pronounced GEH-TOE.) Luther was a religious zealot who thought he was so close to God he would live forever. He also believed the goal of humans was to be perfect. On that point, his son disappointed him. For instance, Charles was physically weak and had a hard time talking. Throughout his childhood, Charles' father would burst into fits of rage — mocking, belittling, and beating his son.

Guiteau wanted so badly to please his father that he took on the same kind of religious beliefs as he grew older. At age 18 he joined a religious group in upstate New York led by his father's religious instructor, John Humphrey Noyes.

Noyes led a small religious community named Oneida. It had about 300 members. These members were allowed, and even encouraged, to have several romantic partners. Even with those kinds of rules, Guiteau had trouble finding anybody interested in him. This was likely because he insisted he was above everybody, that he was chosen by God to be there and that he should be treated better than others. He was, by all accounts, incredibly annoying. As a result, he found himself alone and rejected more than a few times. His nickname among the women of Oneida was "Charles Gitout" (as in "Get OUT!")

After living there six years, Guiteau left in 1865 and attempted to start a religious newspaper. That proved to be more work than he expected, and he gave up after four months, returning for another year to Oneida.

Guiteau's failures were epic in work and in love. After Oneida, in 1869, he married a young librarian named Annie Bunn, whose later descriptions of her four years with him were terrifying. He was violent with her, even locking her in a closet at times. She felt he was "possessed of an evil spirit" and divorced him.

After his failure as a newsman, Guiteau took on work as a lawyer. If you were in any sort of trouble with the law, you did not want Charles Guiteau as your lawyer. Back then, being a lawyer didn't require someone to go to law school and pass a state exam. Guiteau clearly needed a bit of legal education. His work as a lawyer in New York and Chicago quickly became famous for how weird he was in court and how he seemed more interested in preaching religion than defending a client.

During Guiteau's 14 years working as a lawyer, he persistently tried to convince wealthy Chicago citizens to help him buy one of the city's most successful newspapers. He promised to give them great coverage should they run for political office. But he couldn't find a wealthy backer. Perhaps they saw through Guiteau's soaring ego or noted his unsteady personality, or both. Nobody, it seemed, was interested in going into business with him.

Uninterested in law and out of luck when it came to buying a newspaper, he tried making money by returning to religion. Guiteau traveled the country as a preacher. He would arrive in cities, advertise his upcoming appearances, and end up preaching to small groups.

He found little success in this new pursuit. Many listeners heckled him while he spoke or simply walked away.

As he moved through life and its many disappointments, Guiteau remained certain he was somehow meant for a larger purpose. This is likely how he convinced himself that it was OK to cheat landlords — that he was somehow above the law. He wasn't above the law, of course, but he was often out of money. He had a system of staying in fine boarding houses and sneaking out on his last day without paying. Occasionally the law caught up with him. Guiteau spent at least some time in jail for failure to pay in 1874.

As time went on and he needed money, Guiteau began begging family members for loans. His sister was helpful at first, offering not only money but a place to live with her family in Wisconsin. But Guiteau soon enough had his sister fearing for her life. Once he stood near her and raised the ax he had been using to cut wood. She tried to have her brother put into a mental hospital, but he left Wisconsin before she had the chance.

Guiteau roamed from town to town and from boarding house to boarding house.

His further attempts to make money included suing people and organizations including the commune where he lived for years. Claiming he was owed money for the work he did at Oneida, Guiteau threatened to sue Reverend Noyes. But when Guiteau's own lawyer realized Guiteau's reputation for doing very little work, he walked away from the case.

It was Noyes who told Guiteau's father the sad truth: Charles Guiteau was clearly insane. Charles' father and brother were also convinced he should be put away and regretted they did not have the

Roscoe Conkling of New York was a powerful figure in the Republican Party.

money to put him in an asylum.

In 1880, after dodging landlords and others to whom he owed money, Charles Guiteau drifted into Boston. There he became fascinated with politics. He read with great interest about Roscoe Conkling, a rich and powerful senator from New York. It was well known that Conkling could make others rich if they were loyal to him and the Stalwarts. The spoils system, or "machine" politics, was thriving in Washington, D.C.

This, Guiteau thought, would be his way into the fame that he deserved. He quickly decided he would work for the Republican Party and be, like Conkling, a Stalwart.

He took a great interest in the upcoming presidential election and made sure he got himself into as many campaign meetings and rallies as possible. He desperately hoped to make a name for himself among the powerful leaders of the Republican party, believing he would eventually be given an important job with the government.

Three days after Garfield was selected as the Republican candidate for president, Guiteau went to New York to campaign on his behalf and hand out copies of a speech he had written in Boston praising Garfield. He frequently approached Chester Arthur, offering him copies of the speech. A powerful Republican, Arthur at one point agreed to let Guiteau deliver the speech at a small gathering in New York. In this, his only delivery of the speech, Guiteau choked — talking for only a few minutes and claiming it was too hot.

Guiteau nonetheless carried copies of the speech, handing them out to Republican Party leaders he met. He insisted the speech helped Garfield win the presidential election of 1880. Guiteau, in fact, believed the new president would be so grateful

A magazine caricature of Guiteau after his arrest

for Guiteau's speech and help with the campaign that he would give Guiteau exactly the job he wanted. He wished to be an American ambassador — a consul — to Paris, France.

That was, after all, how the political machine worked. The problem was, Garfield intended to stop the spoils system. He wanted to give jobs to people who could perform them well, not to those who did him favors.

With Garfield in the White House, Guiteau moved to Washington, D.C., convinced the new president would appoint him to the job he sought. But Guiteau would have to wait a while. A LOT of people wanted jobs.

Garfield's first months as president were spent making appointments to more than 800 government jobs. Guiteau went to the White House at least 15 times, waiting to speak with the new president or his secretary of state, James Blaine, to discuss the Paris job. If he was told to wait or treated in a way he disliked, Guiteau would explain his importance. He would announce that his speech had won the election for Garfield.

In this time, as in so many others, Guiteau's attempts to impress important people simply backfired. One senator later said he would not have recommended this strange man for any job. "I treated him as kindly and as politely as I could," the senator said, "but I was very desirous of getting rid of him."

Guiteau eventually was granted a brief meeting with President Garfield. One on one with the president, Guiteau explained his support, offering the president a copy of his published speech. On the cover, Guiteau had written "Paris Consulship" and his name.

Guiteau left the meeting confident he'd get the job. He continued visiting the White House, walking among visitors, staff, and others. He was drawing attention to himself but not in the way he'd hoped. At one point he attended a public function — a reception at the presidential mansion — and walked up to the first lady, introduced himself, and handed her his business card.

After politely dealing with dozens of encounters with Guiteau at the State Department, Secretary of State Blaine finally told him the truth. He said Guiteau had "no prospect whatsoever" of receiving the Paris job from the president.

For the next several months, Guiteau remained in Washington, D.C. He was friendless, broke, and continually writing to the president with suggestions, including that he get rid of Blaine. By this time, Guiteau had been banned from the White House over his odd behavior, and his continued letters were placed in what was basically an "ignore" folder.

Guiteau would say, during his trial and imprisonment, that it was two months after meeting with Garfield that he first heard an instruction from God. According to Guiteau, the voice of God told him Garfield needed to be "removed" from office and Guiteau needed to make it happen with a gun.

Garfield was presented to voters as the candidate for honesty in government

CHAPTER 8
A POLITICAL MESS

In seeking to win the presidency of 1880, James Garfield had two major issues on his mind. One was a result of his own upbringing: to take care of the working people in the country, especially those who until recently had been enslaved. He was also determined to undo what he saw taking place throughout his career in Congress: a political system that allowed many men to become rich and powerful for the wrong reasons.

Neither of these ideas was going to go over well with everyone in his own party. But Garfield was a man of honor and vision, and his time was a challenging one for anyone who wanted to change a system that was heading in the wrong direction.

That system of dishing out good jobs or other favors to loyal "friends" was called the spoils system. The name came from the saying "to the victor go the spoils," meaning that the winner of a war gets to enjoy all the riches and comforts that used to belong to the enemy — money, land, possessions, etc.

When political candidates won office in the early and mid-1800s, they usually made sure to reward the loyal party members who helped them get elected.

In the years that Garfield was a U.S. senator, he saw how these spoils meant giving good jobs to people who didn't deserve them and knew very little about the work involved. The spoils system wasn't necessarily illegal. Presidents were given the power to appoint whomever they pleased. But too often jobs went to friends and supporters, not qualified people who would help the country thrive.

At that time, money was flowing into the U.S. economy in levels never seen before. Outside of government, the growth of factories and the Industrial Revolution brought rapid change to the United States. It was hard to keep cities clean, and it was hard to keep rich men and government leaders honest.

And as industry grew and factories rose, the owners of those industries found themselves in a world of riches that few could imagine. In desperate need of jobs, poor people found opportunities to work. The rush to these factories resulted in dramatic growth in the number of Americans living in cities.

Factories were running hard while the workers in them were forced to work long days (10- or 12-hour days were typical) in often unsafe and unhealthy conditions. This caused little concern from the factory owners, who kept the bulk of the money to themselves and made sure they contributed to their government officials to ensure favors in the future. The workers who were putting in such long hours? They had no power to complain, and they would lose their jobs if they did.

These were the people Garfield thought of when he entered

government and when he fought against unfair practices. His own experience with poverty had inspired him to run for office in the first place. He'd hoped to make a difference for the working people of America. Those were people who were not rich and did not have powerful friends handing out money and favors. In other words, most Americans.

Garfield knew full well what hard-working people in America had to put up with just to survive. He need only remember his mother's hard work raising his family to understand the difficulty so many families faced. Because of this, he took his role as a senator quite differently from those who saw the U.S. Congress as a place to swing deals and reward friends. He'd entered political office with hopes of helping make the country a good place for everyone, no matter their wealth.

It bothered him that the country, which held such promise and had given him so much opportunity, was being soured by politicians who were creating laws to serve the wealthy class and its friends. It was as though you were either in or out of the club. Most people were out, and the club took care if its own.

By the time Garfield's name was mentioned in the presidential contest, the Republican Party had become divided over the spoils system. Those Republicans calling themselves Stalwarts wanted not only to keep the spoils system in place; they were also against making peace with the southern states in the long aftermath of the Civil War. The spoils system benefitted the Stalwarts, and it benefitted companies that helped them financially. Regular Americans worked hard for very little while lawmakers and their rich friends kept the money at the top.

The Stalwarts presented an incredibly strong force in the party. In fact, when President Rutherford B. Hayes criticized the spoils system, Stalwarts made work miserable and difficult for him. Hayes decided he would refuse to accept nomination for a second term, claiming the whole thing "embarrassing."

In search of a replacement, the Stalwarts wanted former president Ulysses S. Grant. Considered an American hero for leading the Union Army in the Civil War, Grant also allowed — willingly or not — lots of corruption. During his time in the White House, the spoils system flourished.

Nowhere did the spoils system show its true colors more than in New York City. New York was the home state of Senator Roscoe Conkling, somebody who rose through the spoils system to become one of the most powerful men in the country. He had worked hard years earlier to help Ulysses Grant win the presidency, and Grant appointed Conkling one of the most prized positions. He put him in charge of the New York Customs House. And Grant appointed Conkling's best friend, Chester Arthur, as head collector of the Customs House.

In this time before the government collected income tax, it leaned heavily on import fees. About 70 percent of all imports coming into America came into this New York building and required fees. The goods going through this one building were responsible for one-third of the money that supported the U.S. government.

Conkling could appoint whomever he pleased to any of the high-paying jobs at the Customs House. And he could demand in return their loyalty in money and votes for him and the Republican Party. He enjoyed this position, and used it to great advantage. Naturally, in

In this cartoon, Garfield is shown wrangling crooked politicians.

1880 he originally wanted Grant to get the Republican nomination.

A different group of Republicans, those known as the Half-Breeds, stood up to the Stalwarts and called for reform. These two groups battled it out during the 1880 convention in Chicago that, when all was said and done, chose Garfield as the nominee. And how Garfield dealt with the spoils system as president showed his backbone and determination for fairness.

★ ★ ★

Meanwhile in the South, troubles continued for former slaves who had been freed by President Lincoln's Emancipation Proclamation and by the 13th amendment in 1865. Fifteen years later, these free people faced violence when they attempted to vote in elections or to exercise other basic freedoms.

Garfield did not make many campaign speeches, but his most significant one took place in front of 50,000 people in New York. He spoke about the need to treat black Americans with the respect they deserved. Recalling the Civil War, he said no black man was a traitor and no Union solider was ever betrayed by a black man anywhere. He felt he needed to speak out about this. Many white Americans, it seemed, had stopped caring about issues faced by black Americans now that the Civil War was finished and slavery was forbidden. But Garfield knew that although slavery was over, black people were anything but safe in the Southern states. Killings, beatings, and other violence continued against African Americans by angry southerners still upset over losing slavery.

Former slave and anti-slavery leader Frederick Douglass spoke to a massive gathering in October 1880. He insisted to his largely black audience that Garfield "must be our next president" as he understood the difficulties of black American lives after the Civil War. Because of Garfield's own beginnings, he could understand and address issues of homelessness and poverty. "He has shown us how man in the humblest of circumstances can rise, win," Douglass said.

Garfield knew that southern blacks would be threatened with violence when they sought to vote. Assuming he'd lose Southern

Frederick Douglass

states as a result, he realized he'd have to win New York. That's why he needed to be on the good side of Roscoe Conkling. The party chose Conkling's friend Chester Arthur to be Garfield's running mate. Arthur had never held office. It was a move Garfield was not happy about but knew he needed to accept.

And that move worked. Conkling felt confident he would be able to keep his role at the Customs House. He threw his support behind Garfield, who won the November 1880 election by a very close margin.

Garfield was sworn into office March 4, 1881. The early days of his presidency were filled with interviewing people who sought jobs in the administration. They were seeking many positions that, in the past, would have gone to an incoming president's friends and supporters.

When Conkling visited the president, he expected to be told he would continue to run the Customs House. But Conkling received some bad news. Garfield decided against putting him in charge of the Customs House. The president explained that his choosing Chester Arthur as his running mate had been his gesture of gratitude to Conkling. The senator was furious, and Garfield expected as much. "I owe something to the dignity of my office," Garfield explained to a friend.

Public response to the decision seemed to agree with Garfield, but Conkling wasn't finished. Vice President Arthur, still more loyal to Conkling than the president, argued against Garfield's decision. Arthur even signed protest petitions against the president.

Then Conkling took a gamble he surely later regretted: He quit the U.S. Senate as a public protest against the president. He did so with the assumption that the New York Legislature — in charge of electing senators back then — would vote to bring him back. Thus, Conkling figured, he would have made his point by walking out on the president only to be voted back in by the New York Legislature.

Garfield basically scoffed at the move, calling it a weak attempt at

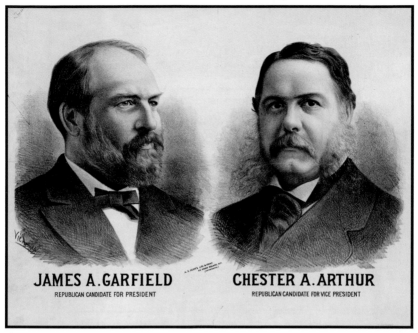

JAMES A. GARFIELD
REPUBLICAN CANDIDATE FOR PRESIDENT

CHESTER A. ARTHUR
REPUBLICAN CANDIDATE FOR VICE PRESIDENT

Garfield accepted Arthur as his vice presidential candidate, but the two were not cut from the same cloth.

drama. More and more people agreed. One congressman claimed it was a "great big baby boohooing because he can't have all the cake."

Conkling's plan backfired. He was never elected back into the Senate. His power was slipping dramatically. His only connection to power was in Chester Arthur, a man who in a few months, would be president.

Charles Guiteau expected his crime to be celebrated

CHAPTER 9
GUITEAU'S CRIME

On May 18, 1881, Charles Guiteau believed God was speaking to him — and telling him to kill the president of the United States. That's what Guiteau would claim many months later. Guiteau insisted to his jailers, his jury, and anybody else who would listen in the meantime that he had heard the voice clearly tell him what to do. The voice said the new president needed to be out of the way for the Republican Party to succeed. This voice came to Guiteau not long after he received bad news. He was told that his hope of the new president giving him a job was not going to happen.

Imagine a mind already unable to sort out fantasy from reality. Imagine a life of constant high hopes met with constant failure. Now add to that a big dose of anger and embarrassment. What does it add up to? In Guiteau's head, it led not only to a voice telling him to kill the president, but convincing him it was a good idea for the country.

He also believed that, after the killing, he would be thanked by a grateful nation.

"(Garfield) has proved a traitor to the men that made him," Guiteau wrote in a letter to be read after the assassination. "This is not murder, it is a political necessity. This will make my Friend Arthur president and save the Republic. I expect president Arthur and Sen. Conkling will give the nation the finest administration it has ever had."

In his criminally crazed mind, he didn't have much room for the idea that he might get into some trouble for killing the president. He figured he'd be arrested and jailed for a while, sure. But he also planned on getting pardoned and thanked by would-be President Chester Arthur.

Once Guiteau was convinced to move ahead with the murder, he considered how and when to do it. He also spent lots of time thinking about all the fame and publicity it would bring. He even started to re-write an old book he had published during his unsuccessful days as a preacher. Once he was famous, he figured, the book would probably be in high demand. He had titled it, "The Truth: A Companion to the Bible."

Needing a weapon for his deed, Guiteau borrowed money and bought what at the time was a very expensive pistol. He picked that pistol not because it would deliver a better shot, but because it looked good. That was only proper, he thought, for something that was sure to become a national treasure.

Oddly, as Guiteau was planning his crime, he continued to write letters to President Garfield. He wrote to urge Garfield to give in to Roscoe Conkling's demands. The president never wrote back.

Guiteau found himself with plenty of opportunities to kill Garfield before the day he pulled the trigger. He had made it a practice of following the First Couple to various events, once coming close to shooting the president during a church service. Guiteau knew he could find Garfield regularly at the Vermont Avenue Christian Church. That was where Garfield had attended since coming to Washington as a Congressman. Before his presidency, Garfield had taught Sunday school there and pitched in to work when the church needed a bigger building. Armed with his gun, Guiteau attended a service and sat behind the president. The president was unprotected. Guiteau had his chance. For whatever reason, he chose not to shoot the president then. Instead he shouted at the preacher during the service.

Today it would be unthinkable for the president of the United States to stroll on his own down a street on his way to church or a restaurant. In 1881, however, the idea of a protecting the president's every move was seen as unnecessary. Even though a previous president, Abraham Lincoln, had been killed by an assassin, that crime was viewed largely as a shocking result of the Civil War. People didn't think such a thing would happen again, especially during times of relative peace.

After all, the American system of government allowed for the country to get rid of an unpopular or bad president peacefully — by voting him out. No need for bloodshed, storming a castle, or overthrowing someone who would otherwise cling to power for life. The United States — a little more than 100 years old at the time — had a system that put the head of the government up to vote every four years.

Guiteau, a tragic bug in that system, had read in the newspaper of the president's plan to travel to visit his wife at their New Jersey home on July 2. That morning, Guiteau woke early. After a walk in Lafayette Park, he went to the Baltimore and Potomac Railroad Station and waited.

In addition to his gun, he carried two letters with him. One was to William Tecumseh Sherman, chief of the army, and the other was addressed to the White House. In the letter to Sherman, Guiteau explained in a series of short sentences that he was going to jail for shooting the president and would like Sherman to order his troops to take over the jail. In the letter to the White House, he wrote with calm logic, explaining that he was doing what needed to be done. He called Garfield's death a "sad necessity," but one that was needed to save the Republican Party and save the country. He wrote with a chilling, matter-of-fact tone that Mrs. Garfield would be better off this way, rather than watching her husband die of natural causes. Since Garfield was a Christian, wrote this failed preacher, he'd be happier in heaven than on Earth.

Guiteau arrived at the train station around 8:30 a.m. Within an hour President Garfield and Secretary of State Blaine arrived. No bodyguards were present, of course, just an assistant carrying their bags.

The three walked several steps into a carpeted waiting room before Guiteau approached from behind the president. Standing just three feet away, Guiteau fired his first shot. It grazed Garfield's arm, and the president shouted, "My God, what is this?" As the president began to turn around, Guiteau fired a second shot that pierced Garfield's back just above the waist. The president fell forward, the back of his gray summer suit darkening with blood as onlookers rushed to make sure Guiteau didn't escape.

No bodyguard was on hand to keep Guiteau away from the president.

Witnesses said the look on Guiteau's face went from serious while taking the first shot to terrified after taking the second. As the president fell, Guiteau made a run toward an exit door. One bystander blocked his way out, and as Guiteau ran for another door, a ticket agent grabbed him and held on, shouting, "This is the man." Police already at the station kept Guiteau from the hands of an angry crowd. Guiteau told the police, "I want to go to jail."

Garfield was in agonizing pain, and it wasn't going to get better. The first doctor to treat the president was Dr. Smith Townsend, the city's health officer. Garfield was not at death's door. His wounds seemed serious but not devastating. In fact, he would remain alive for several months, and he likely would have survived the shooting entirely were it not for poor medical care. The president's poor care began with Townsend inserting his fingers into Garfield's back wound to search for the bullet.

Neither Townsend nor the doctor who would take over Garfield's care were concerned about germs. The science of germs and infections was new, and Garfield's doctors from start to finish were not believers.

In an eerie coincidence, Robert Todd Lincoln, whose father had died from an assassin's bullet years earlier, was at the train station when Garfield was shot. Lincoln brought to the scene the same doctor who tended to Abraham Lincoln's shooting. That man was Dr. Willard Bliss.

Bliss, who had been a war surgeon during the Civil War, took over Garfield's care from that day forward. He began by moving the president from the station to the White House. While Guiteau alone committed the crime, Bliss would someday share blame for Garfield's death. The doctor allowed few others to treat Garfield and resisted any other medical opinions on his care.

Bliss certainly didn't bother giving any time to the idea that germs could cause problems. The doctor didn't understand the need for sterile tools and a clean wound. In this, he wasn't alone. Many, if not most, U.S. doctors at the time still rejected the idea of tiny germs causing big problems.

That discovery had come about in the mid-1860s by a Scottish surgeon named Joseph Lister. (He's the namesake of Listerine mouthwash, which famously "kills germs that cause bad breath.") He believed germs played a role in patients' getting worse during surgery, that germs in the air and elsewhere were making their way into the open wounds. Lister experimented in surgeries by spraying

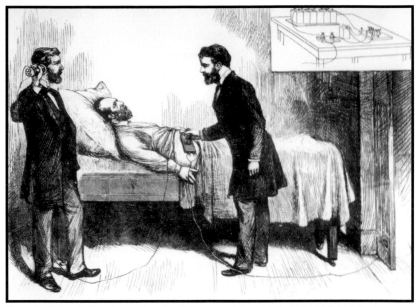

Alexander Graham Bell used a new invention of his to search for the bullet in Garfield's body, but he was advised to search in the wrong area.

disinfectant over the patient and wound during the operations. Infections in these circumstances went way down. Over time, of course, this became accepted science.

But the world of medicine would not change soon enough for James Garfield. His doctor thought this was a silly idea, getting an infection from something you couldn't even see.

After the shooting, days passed and the president struggled to stay alive. In a rush to help, inventor Alexander Graham Bell offered his latest invention — a metal detector — to help locate the bullet in Garfield's back. Dr. Bliss was so sure of himself that he allowed only the president's right side to be examined. He was convinced that's where the bullet would be found. It was not there.

For weeks the public watched and waited, learning of the president's health updates through the newspapers. There were high hopes, then low ones. On September 6, Garfield was taken by a special train to his summer seaside cottage in New Jersey. There, it was hoped, the ocean breeze might help his condition. It didn't. On September 19, at 10:35 p.m., the president died.

An autopsy showed that the bullet was indeed lodged within the left side of Garfield's body. That was, of course, the opposite of what Bliss thought. There was a long, open path through the right side of Garfield's body. Bliss had assumed this was caused by the bullet. But the wound was determined to have been caused by fingers and instruments used in searching for the bullet.

Doctors also discovered that much of Garfield's body — his ears, the middle of his back, his shoulders, and his kidney area — were all poisoned with infections. He even had pneumonia in both of his lungs. Infection is what ultimately killed Garfield. The bullets started his problems, but they alone could not have killed him.

In her book on Garfield, biographer Candice Millard wrote: "It became immediately and painfully apparent that, far from preventing or even delaying the president's death, his doctors very likely caused it."

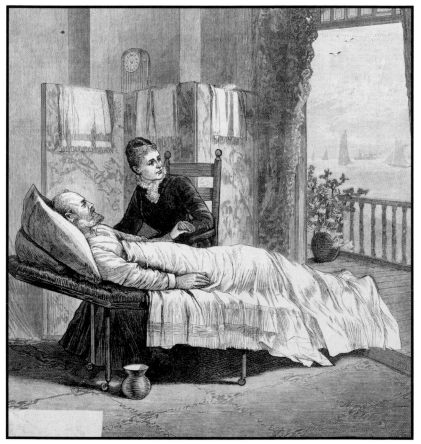

Garfield's final days were spent on the seashore in New Jersey.

A cartoon depicted Chester Arthur with a white elephant that resembled Roscoe Conkling, meaning Conkling had become unwanted and troublesome to the new president.

CHAPTER 10
THE AFTERMATH OF THE ASSASSINATION

In the end, the death of President James Garfield likely helped accomplish something it may have taken him years to do. In response to the assassination, Congress soon passed a law that got rid of the spoils system.

President Garfield's shooting and eventual death had upset and angered citizens throughout the country. Rich or poor, they questioned how and why something like this could happen. What would motivate such a crime? As Garfield suffered and eventually died, people learned hard truths. Newspapers described the spoils system and how it worked like a big club that did favors for members only. Reports revealed how Charles Guiteau, expecting a nice job from Garfield, went mad when he didn't get it.

Like Garfield, the American people began insisting this system come to an end. They wanted government reform. They wanted politicians who would pledge to seek it as well. The big question was

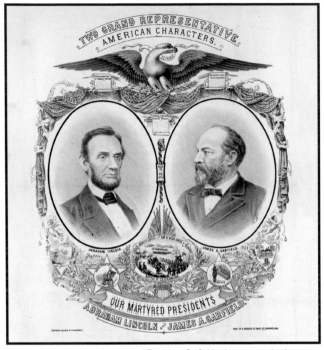

A memorial to President Lincoln and President Garfield, whose assassinations were the first in the country's history and came only 16 years apart.

how the new president, Chester Arthur, would deal with the system that made him so successful. That question was answered quickly. Starting with his first public speech as president, Arthur made clear his support for reform. Then in the 1882 elections, many in Congress who supported the old system were voted out of office.

One year into his presidency, Arthur signed into law The Pendleton Civil Service Act. This law completely changed the system. While government jobs were once given to men based on favors and friendship, the law required that they go to the people who were best for the jobs.

Perhaps nobody was more surprised by Arthur's decision than Roscoe Conkling. No longer in the U.S. Senate, Conkling had to be feeling pretty good now that his old friend was the new president. It was Conkling, after all, who was largely responsible for Arthur becoming vice president and, thus, assuming the presidency after Garfield died. Conkling was ready to have some favors returned.

In a move that would have seemed normal years before, Conkling began telling Chester Arthur what to do. For starters, he wanted Arthur to replace the man who had Conkling's old position of running the New York Customs House. Not that Conkling wanted the job. He wanted something else. He wanted to be appointed Secretary of State.

Conkling, however, got bad news. His old friend was no longer somebody he could push around. Arthur outranked him now and had far more power. Arthur was president of the United States. Arthur denied both of Conkling's requests. Conkling left Washington feeling angry and betrayed. He was so upset that he refused to accept Arthur's offer to place him on the U.S. Supreme Court.

Arthur's actions worked well for him. Those who doubted he would clean up the system were happy to be proven wrong. His popularity rose. His image improved. Still, he did not muster enough support to get re-elected. His own party chose a different candidate. When it came time to nominate a candidate in 1884, the Republicans chose James Blaine (who would lose the presidential election to Democrat Grover Cleveland). Arthur left the office far more popular a figure than when he entered it, and he died two years later at the age of 56.

In November 1881, less than two months after Garfield's death, the trial of Charles Guiteau began. It would stretch into the early days of January 1882. Guiteau's lawyers argued that he was innocent by reason of insanity. They said mental disorders prevented him from thinking straight and knowing right from wrong. The prosecutors, in response, said Guiteau knew full well what he was doing. They said that he knew it was wrong to shoot the president but did it anyway — and should pay the price.

Guiteau behaved horribly at the trial, often yelling and insulting his lawyers or interrupting people giving testimony. During the trial, three dozen medical experts took the stand to talk about insanity and mental illness. It was the jury's job to decide if Guiteau was guilty of knowingly killing the president or if insanity clouded his reasoning and guided his actions.

When it was his turn to testify, Guiteau spent nearly an entire week's time on the stand. He insisted he was instructed by God — the "Deity," in his words — to "remove" Garfield. Asked if he disliked the president, Guiteau said he considered him a "personal and political friend."

"I simply executed what I considered the divine will for the good of the American people," he said. He also explained that if Americans knew better, they would not call Guiteau an assassin, but a patriot.

"I want it distinctly understood that I did not do that of my own personal volition, but on the inspiration of the Deity," he said. "I never would have shot the president on my own personal account."

To which the prosecutor asked, "Who bought the pistol? The Deity or you?"

But Guiteau stubbornly refused to take responsibility for killing Garfield, shifting all blame to the "Deity."

As the trial came to a close and both sides made their best case to the jury, Guiteau himself was allowed to address them. He decided to sing a song — "John Brown's Body" — and warned the jury that if they found him guilty "the nation would pay for it."

That didn't seem to bother the jury. It took less than one hour for them to meet and decide that Guiteau was guilty. The judge sentenced Guiteau to death by hanging. The assassin appealed the decision, even writing to President Arthur and asking for time to appeal to the U.S. Supreme Court. But his fate was sealed. Guiteau was executed at the District Jail in Washington, D.C., on June 30, 1882. Before he was hanged, he read a biblical passage and a poem of his own which ended with, "Glory Hallelujah! Glory Hallelujah! I am with the Lord!"

Not long after Garfield's death, the medical community embraced the work of Joseph Lister. He was the Scottish surgeon who believed germs played a role in patients' failure to recover from wounds or surgery. Many people realized the safer, cleaner procedures might have saved the president's life.

Lister went on to become one of the most admired men in medicine. He was honored by kings and queens. Doctors around the world began using antiseptics in surgery, which dramatically lowered the rate of deaths from infections. In 1902 the American ambassador to England praised Lister at a celebration honoring the doctor. According to the ambassador, Lister deserved to be thanked not only by doctors or by the United States, but "humanity itself."

The same medical community had harsh words for Dr. Bliss. He was accused of botching Garfield's care, particularly when it came to causing infections in the president's wound. Also, American surgeons blamed him for damaging the country's reputation for surgery.

Bliss, however, never admitted doing anything wrong. He shocked Congress when he billed the government $25,000 for his work. (That would be about $500,000 today.) Congress instead offered $6,500, which Bliss angrily refused.

Garfield's goal of cleaning up the spoils system would see movement thanks to Chester Arthur's support of a new civil service law. Civil rights for black Americans, however, would not get much attention from Washington following Garfield's death.

Garfield knew that freed slaves in the South were anything but free. Even after slavery was outlawed and blacks could vote, they were routinely treated miserably in many Southern states, threatened and often killed if they attempted to vote.

Knowing firsthand that education was important to a good life, and that most blacks were illiterate, Garfield recommended a universal education system in which the U.S. government would fund education throughout the country. The idea never made it to Congress.

"Had he lived," wrote a scholar at the University of Virginia's Miller Center, he would have kept the issue "at the forefront of his administration."

Civil rights did not advance during Arthur's presidency. If anything, he went the opposite way by signing into law the Chinese Exclusion Act, which put a 10-year ban on Chinese immigrants, the first such law of its kind. (The concern was that too many Chinese were taking American jobs.)

In the southern states, laws separating blacks from whites in schools, restaurants, transportation, theaters, and other public

Garfield is memorialized with a statue in Cincinnati, Ohio, his home state.

buildings continued through the end of the century. Violence against blacks became a way of life well into the 20th Century.

Although James Garfield did not get the chance to be a great president, he did briefly bring about a shift in the American mood. Because of the kind of man he was, an entire nation — ripped apart by the Civil War mere years earlier — came together to hope for his recovery and to mourn his loss. As one biographer wrote, in the days after his death "his countrymen mourned not as northerners or southerners, but as Americans."

TIMELINE >>>>>>>>>>>>>>>>>>>>>>>>>>

Nov. 19, 1831: James Garfield is born in Ohio; his father dies when James is still an infant, leaving him to be raised in poor conditions by his mother

Sept. 8, 1841: Charles Guiteau is born in Illinois; after his mother dies when Guiteau is 7, he is raised by a violent father

1859: Guiteau enters the Oneida religious sect

1859: Garfield is elected to the Ohio state senate

Nov. 6, 1860: Abraham Lincoln is elected president

April 12, 1861: Southern forces fire on Fort Sumter in South Carolina, and the Civil War begins

August 1861: Garfield leaves his political office and is made a lieutenant colonel in the Union Army, soon promoted to colonel

January 1862: Garfield makes a heroic name for himself by leading a Union triumph at the Battle of Middle Creek and is soon promoted to brigadier general

November 1862: Garfield is elected to the U.S. House of Representatives

Jan. 1, 1863: President Lincoln issues an order freeing slaves in rebel states

Nov. 8, 1864: Lincoln is reelected as president

April 9, 1865: The South surrenders and the Civil War ends

April 15, 1865: President Abraham Lincoln is assassinated

Dec. 6, 1865: The 13th Amendment, abolishing slavery, is approved

1880: Guiteau begins his involvement in Republican Party politics, with hopes of winning favor with party leaders

July 8, 1880: Garfield, a U.S. senator, is chosen as Republican presidential nominee

Nov. 3, 1880: Garfield is elected president of the United States

March 4, 1881: James Garfield is sworn in as president of the United States

July 2, 1881: Guiteau, distraught over not getting an appointment, shoots Garfield in a Washington, D.C., train station

Sept. 19, 1881: Garfield dies after months of ineffective medical care

June 30, 1882: Guiteau, after a trial and verdict of guilty, is executed; he sings a religious song of his own creation on the gallows

President William McKinley

PART III

PRESIDENT McKINLEY'S KILLER AND THE AMERICA HE LEFT BEHIND
THE ASSASSIN, THE CRIME, TEDDY ROOSEVELT'S RISE, AND THE DAWN OF THE AMERICAN CENTURY

Leon Czolgosz, assassin

CHAPTER 11
McKINLEY'S KILLER

The time is the summer of 1901, and the World's Fair is in full swing. Millions of people descend upon Delaware Park in Buffalo, New York, to see the new inventions on display and to enjoy the fair's festivities. Colorful buildings glisten in the sunlight. Canals and waterways meander through the park. Rosebushes line the walkways. But the fair is most spectacular at night, when the grounds and the fair's major attraction — the 389-foot Electric Tower — light up. Crowds ooh and ahh at the sight. It is the early years of electricity, and no one has seen so many lights before. Glowing bulbs line every building and every walkway. The place feels magical. The fair at night transforms into a city of light.

On September 5 another blaze of light spreads across the sky. This time it is brilliant fireworks. And the fireworks spell out a message: Welcome, President McKinley! Chief of Our Nation and Our Empire!

President McKinley addresses a large crowd at the World's Fair.

President William McKinley is on a two-day visit to the World's Fair. He's just several months into his second term as president. He's enjoying enormous popularity after leading the United States to a speedy victory in the Spanish-American War and acquiring the territories of Guam, Puerto Rico, and the Philippines. The World's Fair is called the Pan-American Exposition to celebrate the new territories under U.S. control.

More than 116,000 people gather on the fairgrounds to listen to the president speak. "Expositions are the timekeepers of progress," he says. Crowds cheer during the speech, and he calls for "prosperity, happiness and peace to all our neighbors, and like blessings to all the peoples and powers of earth."

Another roar rises from the crowd, but not everyone is cheering. Zoom in and look at the audience more closely. Standing near the president's podium is a young man, scowling. His face darkens at McKinley's every word. And if you zoom in even closer, you may notice that he has one hand in his pocket. Fingering his gun.

Who is this man with the scaring hatred for McKinley? His name is Leon Czolgosz. (That last name is difficult. Here's a simple way to pronounce it: CHOLE-GOSH.) He has a complicated life story but a simple plan. He intends to shoot and kill McKinley. But the beginning of his story — and of his troubles — goes back more than three decades.

★ ★ ★

Leon Czolgosz was a factory worker who'd led a hardworking life as the son of poor Polish immigrants. He was born in Alpena, Michigan, in 1873. He was one of eight children. His father, Paul, worked hauling lumber on the docks of Lake Huron, making only 30 cents an hour (about $5 an hour in today's money). For four months of the year, he was laid off by the lumber company. He made so little money that the family could barely survive.

When Leon was about 5 years old, the Czolgosz family bought a farm. They were happier on the farm, even though they still had to work hard. But a few years later, tragedy shook the family. Leon's mother, Mary, died in childbirth. Without Mary to take care of the household, Paul decided to move the family back to Alpena, where he could find work. Over the next several years, the family moved around — Michigan to Pennsylvania to Ohio. The Czolgosz children worked in factories and on farms to help support the family. Leon worked too. When he was a young teenager, he got his first job at a glassworks factory near Pittsburgh, Pennsylvania.

Was it even legal for children to work in factories? At that time, the answer was yes. Only a few states had laws against child labor. Factories were happy to hire children. Children had a lot of energy. Plus, factories could pay kids a lot less than adults. And for struggling families, any income a child brought home would help. The situation worked out for everybody — everybody except the children. Days spent working in factories were long, exhausting, and dangerous. Children suffered and toiled all day just to bring home a few cents. Imagine if, instead of sending you off to school each morning, your parents sent you to work at a canning plant or a textile mill. And bear in mind that at the end of a long day, you would have to give all the money you earned to your parents to help feed your siblings. That was the case for millions of American children in the late 1800s.

So Leon spent part of his childhood working. Somehow he continued his schooling until he was 16, which was unusual for poor immigrant children, most of whom dropped out and went to work earlier. Leon's brothers said that he was a good student, so his family didn't take him out of school to work full time.

When the Czolgosz family moved to Cleveland, Ohio, Leon got a job at a wire mill, making steel wire for fences. But in 1893 the U.S. economy collapsed. Wages dropped. Workers at the wire factory went on strike to demand fairer treatment. Leon joined them in the walkout. The wire company responded by firing every worker who'd gone on strike.

Out of work, 20-year-old Leon struggled to make sense of the world. He believed in the American dream. And he'd always been interested in American society and its ups and downs. So he started reading a lot. First he read the Bible front to back. He stopped attending church because he felt the priests left out the most important parts of the Bible.

Then he read a book called *Looking Backward* by Edward Bellamy. The novel is about a man named Julian West who goes to sleep in 1887 and wakes up in the year 2000. In the story's version of the future, social classes do not fight with each other but instead work together. The novel struck a chord with Czolgosz. He was upset by the way the poor were treated by the wealthy upper class. He felt the wealthy took advantage of the poor. And he concluded that the wealthy and poor should work together to make life better for everyone.

Six months after being fired, Leon decided to try to get his job back at the wire mill. He knew he was on a list of strikers who'd been dismissed. His old boss, however, had moved on. The new boss wouldn't recognize him. So Czolgosz walked in the door and introduced himself as Fred Nieman. Fred was a family nickname for him. Nieman was easier to pronounce than Czolgosz, and it means "nobody" in German. His scheme worked. He got his job back.

Around this time Leon started joining groups that talked about social issues. He grew increasingly upset by the low wages that his job offered. He hated how big businesses made money but workers remained poor. He hated capitalism, which allowed the gap between rich and poor to widen.

His life was soon disrupted by illness. He couldn't breathe very well, and his heart kept beating rapidly. He visited doctors several times and took several medications that didn't seem to help. No one knows what illnesses he suffered from — or whether they were real or imagined. In 1898 he quit his job. He holed up in his family's house, barely speaking to anyone, especially not his stepmother. He spent his time sleeping and reading publications about politics and social issues. Isolated and ill, the young Czolgosz developed an interest in anarchy, an idea that seemed to fascinate political outsiders and downtrodden people in that era.

What is anarchy? The word is Greek for "no ruler." Anarchy is basically belief in a society without government or law. Anarchists in Czolgosz's time railed against governments and monarchies (nations run by kings and queens).

The ideas of anarchy were exciting to Leon. He became especially interested in the lectures and writings of Emma Goldman. She was a Russian immigrant living in the United States and a strong supporter of anarchy. She gave passionate, fiery speeches against authority. Her speeches drew crowds of thousands. Leon went to Chicago to one of her speeches. In that speech she stated that anarchists must gain their goals by intelligence, not by violence. But then she said that violence was sometimes understandable. Sometimes people couldn't sit around while wrongs were inflicted upon them.

Anarchists like Emma Goldman believed that all authority should be eliminated. And, in the 1890s, some anarchists started taking matters in

Emma Goldman

their own hands. A string of killings and other violent events played out in Europe and North America:

1886, Haymarket Square, Chicago. Culprit: unknown. Crime: Someone throws a bomb at Chicago police, who are there to break up a workers' protest. Death toll: Seven police officers, four civilians. Convicted: Eight anarchists.

1893, Spain. Culprit: Santiago Salvador, anarchist. Crime: Salvador throws explosives into a theater filled with rich people. Death toll: About 20.

1893, France. Culprit: Auguste Vaillant, anarchist. Crime: Vaillant throws a small bomb into the French Parliament. No one is killed, but Vaillant is executed for the deed. Vaillant's last words: "Long live anarchy!"

1894, Lyons, France. Culprit: Cesare Santo, anarchist. Crime: Santo wraps a newspaper around a dagger. He approaches the carriage of French president Sadi Carnot and stabs him. Death toll: One — Sadi Carnot.

1897, Spain. Culprit: Michele Angiolillo, anarchist. Crime: Angiolillo goes to a bath resort where Spanish prime minister Canovas del Castillo is staying and shoots him. Death toll: One — Canovas del Castillo.

1898, Switzerland. Culprit: Luigi Lucheni, anarchist. Lucheni walks up to Empress Elisabeth of Austria and pretends to stumble into her. He stabs her with a concealed knife. Death toll: One — Empress Elisabeth.

These violent acts frightened citizens worldwide. But Leon Czolgosz was not frightened. Instead he was fascinated. To him, violence seemed the only way to bring down unfair systems of government. Czolgosz believed the words of German anarchist Johann Most, who said, "Violence is justified against tyranny and tyrants."

In the spring of 1898, protests erupted in Italy over the rising price of bread. King Umberto I silenced the protests by placing the country under military control. The military fired a cannon into a crowd in Milan, killing more than 100 people.

Far away in New Jersey, an Italian immigrant and anarchist named Gaetano Bresci heard about the massacre. Enraged, he plotted to somehow kill the king. He said goodbye to his family and set off for Italy.

On July 29, 1900, King Umberto had just gotten into his royal carriage when a tall man pushed through the crowd. The man was Gaetano Bresci, all the way from New Jersey. Bresci drew his pistol and fired three shots at the surprised king. Umberto died, and Bresci was arrested.

In Ohio, Leon Czolgosz read of King Umberto's assassination in the newspaper. He carefully cut out the article and folded it into his wallet. Umberto's murder had given him an idea — a deadly, gruesome idea that would change America's future. He decided that he, too, would take matters into his own hands. He would kill President William McKinley.

The assassination of Italy's King Umberto I was part of a wave of political violence.

William McKinley won election in 1896 and reelection in 1900.

CHAPTER 12
A POPULAR PRESIDENT

Who was William McKinley? What did he do to incur such wrath? He was a popular president, so why did Leon Czolgosz feel the desire to kill him? Did McKinley deserve blame for the trouble of the poor and jobless? Or did he just happen to be in the wrong place at the wrong time? Was he a mere symbol of the government that anarchists wanted to bring down?

William McKinley was born in 1843 in Niles, Ohio, to a middle-class family. Niles was a rural town, and young William loved to roam the nearby woods, slosh about in Mosquito Creek, and fly his kite. He attended school in a one-room schoolhouse. He was a hardworking student and always wanted to be at the top of his class. He attended college briefly and then became a schoolteacher. Then the Civil War began.

McKinley admired President Abraham Lincoln, and, guided by strong patriotism, he enlisted in the Union Army. Leaving behind his days as a teacher, McKinley quickly became a skilled soldier and was promoted to commissary sergeant. In this role he was in charge of feeding the troops. September 1862 saw the bloodiest one-day battle of the war — the Battle of Antietam. McKinley's unit arrived hours after the battle started. The Union soldiers, just over the hill, were hungry and thirsty. To reach them with supplies, McKinley would have to ride right through the battle. The danger was clear, but he was determined. As bullets whizzed and cannons blasted, McKinley raced his wagon directly into enemy fire. The Union soldiers cheered as McKinley and the wagon of goods arrived, somehow unharmed.

One man took particular notice of McKinley's bravery. That man was Rutherford B. Hayes, a senior officer in McKinley's regiment. Hayes became a mentor to McKinley. After the war McKinley became a lawyer, and he aspired to become involved in politics. Hayes helped McKinley's budding political career, and they both ended up in Washington, D.C. Hayes was sworn in as U.S. president in 1877, and McKinley became one of Ohio's representatives in the U.S. Congress. As a lawmaker he authored the McKinley Tariff, which put a high tax on imported goods. The tax was meant to protect U.S. industry from foreign competitors.

McKinley married Ida Saxton in 1871, and the couple had two daughters. One died as a baby, and the other died at age 3. The children's deaths sent Ida into a deep depression. She never recovered. She also developed epilepsy, a condition that causes seizures. McKinley was devoted to her and constantly tended to her.

McKinley's devotion to his wife was one quality that made voters love him. After running as a Republican (the party of Lincoln), he served as the governor of Ohio from 1892 to 1896. In 1896 he ran for president of the United States.

The McKinley campaign promised to boost the U.S. economy and raise the country's stature around the world.

McKinley's campaign for president was backed by "big money." His supporters included multimillionaires such as Andrew Carnegie and John D. Rockefeller. His opponent, Democrat William Jennings Bryan, campaigned for the working class. But McKinley also could proclaim his support for the working class. As governor he had protected worker safety and workers' unions.

McKinley did all his campaigning from his home. He sat on his front porch in Canton, Ohio, giving speeches and welcoming visitors. He made himself available to voters every day of the week except Sunday. The economic crash of 1893 had weakened the U.S.

economy and put many people out of work. McKinley promised to further tax all goods imported from other countries. This, he promised, would help American industries grow.

McKinley won the election by a wide margin. He immediately set about trying to repair the economy. His business-friendly presidency helped "trusts" to develop. A trust is a large combination of corporations. Because there is little or no competition, trusts can charge high prices for their products. They can make a heap of money this way. The Standard Oil Company was one trust that had bought out most of its smaller competitors and gained almost complete control of oil production and sale.

You can see why McKinley's ideas would upset poor, working-class Americans like Leon Czolgosz. But large corporations also employed lots of people and helped the economy. Plus, McKinley's import taxes helped American industries, putting people back to work.

And something else was about to make McKinley more popular — a victorious war.

★ ★ ★

At the time Cuba was in trouble. Since 1895 Cuba had been engaged in a struggle for independence from Spain. Across the United States, newspapers told of the horrific measures the Spanish were using to put down the rebellion. Hundreds of thousands of civilians were forced from their homes. Many Americans thought the United States should help Cuba fight for independence. Plus the United States would gain Spain's territories if the U.S. won, making the nation more powerful. President McKinley, however, was hesitant

The damaged USS Maine

to go to war with Spain. He resisted calls to fight until the U.S. naval ship USS *Maine* mysteriously exploded and sank in a Cuban harbor.

McKinley had sent the USS *Maine* to Havana, Cuba, to ensure the safety of American citizens there. On the night of February 15, 1898, an explosion ripped through the front of the ship. The USS *Maine* sank quickly. More than 260 American seamen died.

No one knew what caused the explosion. But many people thought Spain was to blame. Calls for war grew louder, and this time, McKinley listened. In April he sent troops to Cuba in support of its independence. On April 25 the United States Congress officially declared war on Spain.

The fighting didn't last long. Spain was not very well prepared, and its military was soundly defeated at Manila Bay in the Philippines and at San Juan Hill in Santiago, Cuba. And, after the war, one soldier emerged as a hero — a man named Theodore Roosevelt.

Roosevelt was the Assistant Secretary of the Navy and a strong supporter of going to war with Spain. When the fighting began, Roosevelt resigned from his job in order to organize a volunteer regiment. He gathered men from the southwest United States. He figured they were used to a hot climate like what they would encounter in Cuba. He enlisted ranchers, cowboys, gamblers, American Indians, college athletes, and hunters. The group was varied, but they all had a few things in common: They were sharpshooters and skilled horseback riders. The regiment was dubbed the Rough Riders.

Clad in blue flannel shirts, brown pants, boots, and slouchy hats, 1,060 Rough Riders set off for Cuba. They landed near the Spanish-held city of Santiago and advanced on the city. On July 1, 1898, Roosevelt himself led the Rough Riders on a dramatic charge. The Spanish retreated, and just a few days later, they surrendered.

The Treaty of Paris, signed in December, officially ended the war. Cuba gained its independence, and Spain signed over Guam and Puerto Rico to the United States. The treaty also allowed the U.S. to purchase the Philippines. With control of these islands in the Caribbean Sea and far off in the Pacific, the United States was now an empire.

Riding high on the successes in his first term, McKinley entered the election of 1900 feeling confident. His vice president, Garret Hobart, had died in late 1899, so McKinley would need a new running mate to share the Republican 1900 ticket. The Republican Party chose the Rough Rider hero, Theodore Roosevelt.

And who was McKinley up against? His opponent was the same as in the last election, William Jennings Bryan.

"McKinley Was Right!" a campaign poster proclaimed. McKinley's message focused on the economic growth the nation had experienced during his first term, as well as the worldwide admiration by winning the Spanish-American War. "Prosperity at home, prestige abroad!" was McKinley's slogan. With Roosevelt, he had a national war hero at his side to emphasize his successes and promote his ideas.

Theodore Roosevelt was eager to join the fighting in the Spanish-American War.

McKinley won once again, crushing William Jennings Bryan in the count of electoral votes. He entered his second term with high hopes. A new century was underway. The Buffalo World's Fair — held in the summer and autumn of 1901 — celebrated the U.S. victory over Spain and the dawning of the American empire. A fireworks display arced across the sky, welcoming McKinley to Buffalo.

As he spoke to the crowd, President McKinley had no idea that not everyone was happy to see him. He did not suspect that one man in the masses meant to kill him.

Giant steel factories became a symbol of the Industrial Revolution.

CHAPTER 13
TIMES OF CHANGE

In the last half of the 1800s, industrial growth spread across the United States. This period was known as the American Industrial Revolution. New railroads crossed the country from the Atlantic Ocean to the Pacific. People no longer had to travel long distances in wagons pulled by beasts of burden. They could travel more quickly from one place to another. People could also connect with others far away without traveling at all, after Alexander Graham Bell invented the telephone in 1876. A few years later, Thomas Edison perfected his light bulb. In the following years, electric lights sparkled in the windows of houses and buildings. Street lamps glowed, lighting the way.

More startling and life-changing inventions followed. The first automobiles were produced in the 1870s and 1880s. Although automobiles didn't become widely made or used until the early 1900s, everyone knew big changes in transportation were coming. Other innovations included motion pictures (also known as movies), which awed crowds at public screenings.

Perhaps one of the most important changes that affected many Americans came in manufacturing. Before the Industrial Revolution, most goods were made at home or at small home businesses, using hand tools or small hand-powered machines. The process was slow. But the invention of large machines, powered by steam engines, moved manufacturing of goods to big factories. Goods could be produced quickly and in large quantities. Textile mills sprang up throughout the northeastern United States in the mid-1800s. Other mills and factories followed, making paper, iron, steel, clocks, weapons, and many other goods.

People streamed from rural areas into cities to work in factories. The urban population surged. Men, women, children — anyone could work at a factory. But the work wasn't easy. Factory workers toiled long hours for low wages. Many workers, especially women, returned home from a grueling day of work only to face more work — cooking, cleaning, and caring for children.

Many workers lived in crowded urban neighborhoods such as New York City's Little Italy.

Often the children who worked in factories were given dangerous jobs. Because kids were small, they could crawl into huge machines to clean them. Children could also wiggle into mines and small areas where adults couldn't fit. And children were paid very little, sometimes not at all. By 1900, 18 percent of all American laborers were under the age of 16. That means nearly one of every five workers was a kid.

During the Industrial Revolution, waves and waves of immigrants poured into the United States. Most of these immigrants worked in factories. Between 1860 and 1900, 14 million immigrants came to the United States. The Czolgosz family was one such immigrant family.

Andrew Carnegie

Factory workers didn't take home much money. But factory owners did. Consider Andrew Carnegie, for example. In the 1870s he started a steel mill in Pennsylvania. He bought out his rival, Homestead Steel, and formed the Carnegie Steel Company. Then he owned most of the steel operations in the United States. He became one of the richest men in America.

Rivaling Carnegie as the richest man in America was John D. Rockefeller. Rockefeller bought an oil company and later formed Standard Oil, which grew to a staggering size. Standard Oil bought out smaller oil companies and became a powerful trust. Soon Rockefeller controlled 90 percent of the nation's oil.

Were men like Carnegie and Rockefeller bad men, rolling in riches while their workers suffered and toiled for low wages? That's something people still disagree about. In fact, both men had started from the bottom, working for little pay at factories, eventually climbing their way up. When Carnegie finally sold his steel company for $480 million (that's equal to about $13.8 billion today), he gave away almost all of it. His money built museums and libraries around the country.

Some people admired Carnegie and Rockefeller for their rags-to-riches stories. After all, hadn't they achieved the American dream? But others called them "robber barons." They felt men like Carnegie and Rockefeller made money on the backs of the poor. Leon Czolgosz definitely thought so.

Not all factory workers just sat back and took what was given to them — low wages, long hours, and unsafe working conditions. Workers began organizing into unions. Unions demanded fair pay and better working conditions. If companies didn't agree, the workers could walk off the job and go on strike. Some labor strikes ended peacefully with gains for the workers. Many did not.

★ ★ ★

On the banks of the Monongahela River in Pennsylvania stood the Homestead Steel Mill. The mill employed 3,800 workers. Every day thousands of workers bustled to and from work. And in July 1892 the mill became the scene of bloodshed.

In June the steel and iron workers union called for a strike. The manager of the mill, Henry Clay Frick (hired by Andrew Carnegie), locked the union strikers out of the plant. He ordered the construction of barbed wire fences around the property.

The strikers formed a ring around the mill. Frick was determined to bring in other workers. But he would need armed guards to do it.

So he hired the famed Pinkertons — private security guards — to break through the strikers.

On the night of July 5, some 300 Pinkerton agents gathered downriver, armed with rifles. They assembled onto two barges and made their way upriver, hoping to slip into the mill. They could then escort new, non-union workers into to the mill, and it could reopen.

Striking workers clashed with Pinkerton security guards, who moved in to break the strikers' hold on the Homestead mill.

But all did not go according to plan. On the banks of the river near the mill, 10,000 men, women, and children waited. Many were armed. They weren't going to let the Pinkertons in.

The Pinkertons tried to land, and someone fired a shot. (No one knows if it was the Pinkertons or the strikers). The Pinkertons then opened fire into the crowd. The strikers and the Pinkertons battled all day, until the outnumbered Pinkertons at last surrendered. In all, nine strikers and seven Pinkertons were killed, and many more were wounded. Pennsylvania's governor called in the militia. Eight thousand soldiers showed up, and the mill eventually began running again.

And what does all this have to do with Leon Czolgosz? He wasn't there. He didn't battle the Pinkertons. But something happened afterward that affected him.

On July 23 a man named Alexander Berkman attempted to murder Henry Clay Frick, the manager of Homestead Steel. Berkman was an anarchist.

★ ★ ★

Enter the Panic of 1893. No, it was not a horror movie. The Panic was a period of economic depression. The price of wheat dropped in early 1893. Then a large company that produced and sold twine went bankrupt. This triggered economic panic, and people began withdrawing money from banks. Many banks collapsed, and companies went bankrupt. Workers lost their jobs. Eventually about 20 percent of Americans were unemployed. Others suffered lower wages. Workers went on strike, and one such worker was Leon Czolgosz. He was part of the 1894 strike at the steel wire mill where he worked.

The United States didn't have enough gold to pay its debts, so President Grover Cleveland turned to a super-rich investor and banker named J.P. Morgan for help. Morgan supplied the U.S. with gold to pay its debts. In exchange, he received bonds that he could cash in at a later date. (Can you imagine being rich enough to help the United States pay its bills?) Then Morgan got even richer when he eventually cashed in the bonds.

The bailout plan worked. The economy started bouncing back. Banks reopened. Slowly people started getting their jobs back. But unemployment remained high. And across the United States, many workers, farmers, and other people became worried about rich men like J.P. Morgan having control over the government.

Then came the presidential election of 1896: Republican William McKinley vs. Democrat William Jennings Bryan. Bryan ran on an idea called "Free Silver." He said the United States should allow silver to be mined and minted for money in addition to gold. This would help avoid another gold crisis. And it would put more money into circulation. Bryan blamed the United States government for having a limited amount of gold, which limited the money supply, causing the depression.

Rich businessmen like Carnegie, Morgan, and Rockefeller donated money to McKinley's campaign. A man named Mark Hanna ran McKinley's campaign, and Hanna spent five times more money than the Bryan campaign. He brought nearly 750,000 voters to hear McKinley speak from the front porch during the campaign, even arranging for discounted fares on railroads.

The Democrats had a tough challenge that year. Many people blamed Democrat Grover Cleveland for the Panic of 1893. Clearly many voters were not anxious to give another Democrat the White House. Bryan faced an uphill climb, but he had the support of many rural states.

McKinley, on the other hand, had the support of urban areas in addition to the backing of titans of business. He won the election with 51 percent of the popular vote. Bryan received 47 percent of the popular vote. With 271 electoral votes versus Bryan's 176, McKinley had a victory that pleased the so-called robber barons.

McKinley forged ahead and enjoyed presidential successes: The economy continued to grow, and the Spanish-American war victory turned the United States into an empire with territories across the Western Hemisphere. With Theodore Roosevelt at his side, McKinley won a second showdown with William Jennings Bryan in 1900. And that brings us to the Buffalo World's Fair, and the fateful day that changed everything.

President McKinley in Buffalo, delivering his last public speech

CHAPTER 14
THE CRIME

Cannon fire shook the ground. Windows of the train car shattered as one cannon after another blasted through the early evening sky. Ida McKinley gasped and clutched her husband's hand. As usual, President McKinley soothed her. The cannons were welcoming them to Buffalo, a thunderous salute. Throngs of admirers clamored toward the train as it rolled through Buffalo and toward the fairgrounds. At the station, the train slowed to a stop. President McKinley stepped out.

A large crowd had gathered. One certain young man pushed his way toward the front of the onlookers. He carried a revolver in his pocket. And he meant to use it.

But the guards held the crowd back. By the time the young man — Leon Czolgosz, no surprise — got to the front, he'd lost his chance. McKinley was already being shuffled into a carriage bound for the fairgrounds.

Czolgosz would have to try again tomorrow.

★ ★ ★

A week earlier Leon Czolgosz had been far away in Chicago. Out of work, he had been meandering for several months. He was tired of living at home with his family and cruel stepmother. His family was tired of him too. Leon was always asking for money. And he was convinced he was dying.

He thought moving to a warm climate would help him to feel better. He told his brother he wanted to move out West. His brother asked why, and Leon answered, "I can't stand it any longer." Finally the family gathered enough money to get him started on his new life in the West. He left without saying goodbye.

But he didn't go to warmer climes. Instead he went to Chicago and Cleveland, hoping to join anarchist groups. He introduced himself as Fred Nieman (remember Fred "Nobody"?) and asked if they had any secret plots. Immediately the local anarchists dismissed him as a government spy.

Czolgosz continued moving around. While in Chicago again, he saw an interesting newspaper article. The article announced that McKinley was headed to Buffalo, New York, for the Pan-American Exposition. Surely he would tour the fair and give a speech.

That very day Czolgosz bought a train ticket to Buffalo.

★ ★ ★

Czolgosz arrived in Buffalo without a plan. He knew he wanted to show Emma Goldman and the anarchists that he was committed to the cause. But how? After some thinking, it became clear to him. People were converging on Buffalo to see the president. Everyone seemed to be bowing to the great ruler. He made up his mind to kill the great ruler. He would assassinate McKinley. "It was in my heart. There was no escape for me," he said later.

On the day McKinley was due to arrive in Buffalo, Czolgosz went to a hardware store and bought a .32-caliber Iver Johnson revolver, the very same type of gun used in King Umberto's assassination in Italy. Czolgosz still didn't have much of a scheme. His only plan was to follow McKinley around, and surely he'd find the right moment. That evening he went to the train platform at the fairgrounds to wait for McKinley's arrival.

But he'd blown his chance. The crowd was too big. There were too many guards. No matter, though. The president was giving a speech tomorrow. Maybe then he'd get his chance.

★★★

Czolgosz woke early. Today would be the day, he thought. He headed quickly to the fairgrounds, hoping to get a good spot. Other people, excited to see the popular president, were already there. Czolgosz got as close a spot as he could. Then he waited.

President McKinley arrived in an open carriage, his wife at his side. A throng of people cheered as he stepped to the podium. "I am glad to again be in the city of Buffalo," he began.

In the crowd Czolgosz tried to push forward. But the gathering was thick, and he couldn't move an inch. He wondered whether he could possibly shoot the president from such a distance. He decided he had to get closer. But he couldn't move.

As the president spoke, Czolgosz sweated. Someone elbowed him. Another person stepped on his foot. How could he possibly get off a good shot with so many people pushing and shoving? *Now*, he told himself.

But the president's speech ended. Security guards whisked McKinley from the stage.

I'll have another chance, Czolgosz thought. *Tomorrow.*

★ ★ ★

William McKinley wanted to see Niagara Falls. The falls, after all, powered the electricity that lit up the World's Fair. And it was only about an hour from Buffalo. On September 6, the morning after his speech, he got up early and took his usual morning walk. Then he and Ida boarded the train bound for Niagara Falls.

McKinley was stunned by the magnificent falls. He climbed to the highest rock overlooking the falls and gazed at the scenery. Then he and his wife enjoyed a long lunch at a restaurant with a great view.

But time was ticking. McKinley had to be back in Buffalo by 4 p.m. He was scheduled to go to the Temple of Music, where he planned to shake hands with his constituents — the common folk, the typical fairgoers. His personal secretary, George Cortelyou, warned him it was dangerous. But McKinley insisted. He wanted to meet his voters one by one.

McKinley headed back to Buffalo. He had no idea that a man with a gun was waiting for him.

★ ★ ★

Sometime that day Czolgosz saw in the newspaper that the president would be meeting his voters in the Temple of Music at

4 p.m. It was a perfect opportunity.

Leon headed to the Temple. He made sure his gun was loaded, and he wrapped a white handkerchief around his hand to hide the weapon. That way it would look like he had a bandaged hand. He got in line and waited his turn.

★ ★ ★

The Temple of Music filled with sound. An organist played classical songs. People in line chatted with each other. President McKinley wore a huge smile as he greeted each person.

But Leon Czolgosz didn't smile or talk. He simply waited, trying not to look suspicious. He kept his bandaged hand out of sight.

Finally, it was his turn.

McKinley leaned forward with a smile. He reached to shake the young man's hand. Then he noticed the bandage, so he reached for the other hand.

Czolgosz calmly raised the pistol, still wrapped in a white handkerchief, and aimed at McKinley's torso. He fired twice. One bullet slammed into McKinley's chest and the other into his stomach.

A puff of blue smoke rose over the crowd. A stunned and confused McKinley stood still for a split second. What had just happened? Then his cheeks paled. He clutched his chest and lurched backward.

Leon took aim again. But the tall man behind him tackled him and punched him in the neck. Then security guards pounced on him, pummeling him. Fists flew. Shouts rose. Through it all, Czolgosz yelled, "I done my duty!"

And what of McKinley? He was swaying and staggering, blood darkening his white shirt. His secretary, Cortelyou, helped him to a chair. McKinley noticed the young man being beaten to death. "Easy with him, boys!" he ordered.

Guards dragged Leon away. The president noticed the blood now pouring from his stomach. "My wife," he gasped. "Be careful, Cortelyou, how you tell her."

Leon Czolgosz was taken to jail. And President McKinley was carried away in an ambulance. In the ambulance McKinley reached inside his shirt and pulled a bullet from his chest. But there was still another bullet, lodged deep inside his abdomen.

Czolgosz fired twice from close range before a bystander tackled him.

★ ★ ★

In jail, the shooter told police his name was Nieman. Later, though, he admitted his name was Leon Czolgosz. And he seemed proud of what he'd done.

"I am an anarchist," Czolgosz said. "I killed President McKinley because I done my duty. I don't believe in one man having so much service and another man having none."

But little did Czolgosz know that President McKinley wasn't dead. He was, in fact, very much alive. At the hospital doctors tried to find the other bullet still in McKinley's body. But they couldn't get to it.

An invention unveiled at the World's Fair, just blocks away, could have helped. That invention was the X-ray machine. But the doctors hesitated. They weren't sure the X-ray machine was safe to use. So, they sewed up McKinley's wounds, the bullet still inside him. And he seemed likely to recover nicely.

He did, at first. He left the hospital and went back to the rooms where he was staying. Vice President Teddy Roosevelt was on a camping trip to the Adirondack Mountains when the shooting took place. He headed for Buffalo when he heard about the attack, then got word the president was recovering and returned to the mountains.

McKinley spent the next six days in bed, reading and sleeping. Ida sat by his side. He was cheerful and a bit lonely. He just wanted to get back to work. But the bullet still inside him was turning to poison. Gangrene grew around the bullet. And then blood poisoning set in. At 2:15 a.m. on September 14, 1901, President McKinley died.

Now Leon Czolgosz, the assassin, could be charged with murder.

President McKinley's casket in the rotunda of the U.S. Capitol.

CHAPTER 15
THE AFTERMATH

More than 350 miles away, Theodore Roosevelt leaned back, took a bite of his sandwich, and enjoyed the misty view from Mount Marcy, the highest peak in the Adirondack Mountains and one of the most remote areas in New York State. Suddenly a figure appeared through the mist. A park ranger came running toward Roosevelt's group with a telegram in his hand. Roosevelt read it, his stomach turning. "The President is critically ill," the telegram read. "Absolutely no hope."

Stunned, Roosevelt sat down and finished his sandwich. Then he began the long trek down the mountain. At the bottom he received more news. McKinley was certain to die. And he, Roosevelt, would definitely become the next president.

Roosevelt knew he had to reach Buffalo as soon as possible. He traveled all night in a horse-drawn stagecoach in the rain. The trail was steep and winding, and the horses often slipped. But still, the Roosevelt party galloped on toward the nearest rail depot. A train

Czolgosz behind bars

carried him to Buffalo, where he took the oath of office and became the 26th President of the United States, a president unlike any the nation had ever seen.

★ ★ ★

Leon Czolgosz stood no chance. Minutes after the shooting, crowds surrounded the Temple of Music, shouting, "Kill him! Kill him!" In the days following, angry mobs formed at the jail. And when President McKinley died, the cries grew louder. The public wanted him executed for what he'd done.

But first, detectives had to figure out if Czolgosz acted alone, or if he was part of a conspiracy. During questioning, Czolgosz said that Emma Goldman's words "set him on fire."

Authorities immediately arrested Goldman in Chicago. They also arrested more than a dozen who worked for her anarchist newspaper *Free Society*. Goldman declared she had nothing to do with the assassination, but she admired it. She was later released due to lack of evidence against her. Several years later she was deported and sent back to Russia.

Leon Czolgosz was the son of immigrants, and his actions caused public outcry against immigration. People became suspicious of immigrants, especially those who had anarchist or revolutionary ideas. In 1903 Congress passed a law banning immigrants with anarchist backgrounds from entering the country. Fear of anarchy led to various surveillance or spy programs, and the Federal Bureau of Investigation (FBI) was formed in 1908.

During the trial Czolgosz's lawyers defended him by using the insanity plea. They declared that no sane man would attempt to kill the president in broad daylight. Czolgosz had hardly spoken to them, so their case was difficult. And the assassin refused to speak in court. The trial lasted only two days. The jury declared Czolgosz guilty. He was sentenced to death by electric chair.

Czolgosz was transferred to Auburn State Prison in Auburn, New York. Crowds hurled insults as the train carrying Czolgosz passed by. When the train arrived, a mob rushed at him. Guards had to push the crowd back as they dragged him into the prison.

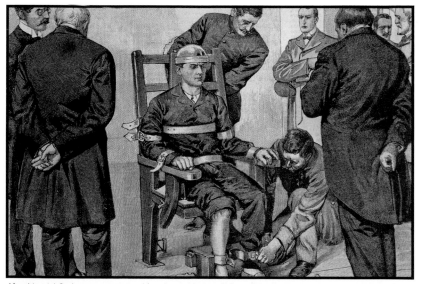

After his trial Czolgosz was executed by electric chair at Auburn Prison, where the first such execution had been carried out about a decade earlier.

Czolgosz was terrified, screaming, "Save me!"

On October 29 the prison warden entered Czolgosz's cell and read him the death warrant. Leon was trembling so violently on the way to the electric chair that guards had to carry him. Once he was strapped in, Czolgosz yelled, "I killed the president for the good of the laboring people, the good people."

★ ★ ★

Teddy Roosevelt, compared to his predecessors, was young, energetic, and athletic. At 42, he became the youngest president in U.S. history. An outdoorsman, he loved to ride horses, hike, and hunt. On one hunting trip, he refused to shoot a bear cub. A toymaker heard the story and began making small stuffed bears. You've probably cuddled one of these. They are called "teddy" bears.

Roosevelt thought the president's mansion needed a name, so he officially dubbed it the White House, which had long been its nickname. He loved to box, and he held boxing matches in his new home. During one bout, he lost his sight in one eye. But that didn't deter him from his visions of the future.

At first he promised to follow McKinley's ideas. But soon it became clear that he was set on reforming government and politics. He didn't stick to the same old way that things had been done for years. He got rid of corrupt officials and appointed young, college-educated people to his administration.

Roosevelt followed his famous mantra, "Speak softly and carry a big stick." That means, in general, not to start conflicts but be able to defend yourself and use force if you have to. He built up the military and turned the U.S. Navy into the best in the world.

Theodore Roosevelt became the youngest person to serve as president, and he approached the job with vigor and determination.

Roosevelt had dreams of expanding trade between the Atlantic and Pacific Oceans. The best way to do that was to build a canal through Central America so ships could pass through, from one ocean to the other. The best site was in Panama. A few years earlier, McKinley's secretary of state, John Hay, had negotiated a treaty to allow for construction of a waterway connecting the oceans. Roosevelt was determined to see the project through. Construction on the Panama Canal began in 1904 and went on for a decade.

Some very rich men were scared of Roosevelt's presidency. Remember Andrew Carnegie and John D. Rockefeller? Those guys weren't exactly excited that he'd come to power. Roosevelt was antitrust, which meant he wanted to break up big industrial corporations — or trusts — and monopolies. Small businesses were suffering, and Roosevelt wanted to change that. His antitrust ideas were the exact opposite of McKinley's. He became a "trust buster" and brought lawsuits against many large corporations.

In 1902 a major coal miner strike shook the country. The mine owners refused to offer higher wages and better conditions, so the miners refused to go back to work. The nation now faced a coal shortage. Teddy Roosevelt stepped in and threatened that the government would take over the coal mines. The mine owners then agreed to meet the miners' requests. This was the first time a president had ever sided with workers rather than owners. Labor reform still had a long way to go, but Roosevelt's intervention turned the tide toward better treatment of workers.

Roosevelt ran for president in 1904 and won easily. One of his first causes in his second term was to ensure food was safe to eat. New laws made sure food, especially meat, was inspected before being sold. This led to the creation of a federal agency called the Food and Drug Administration.

Have you ever taken a spelling test? You can thank Teddy Roosevelt for that. Before his presidency, there was no standard, correct spelling of many words. In 1906 the Simplified Spelling Board was created by a guy we've heard of before — Andrew Carnegie. Carnegie aimed to simplify spelling so English was easier to read and learn. Roosevelt supported the idea and gave an order that the government must use the board's spelling rules.

Some of Teddy Roosevelt's greatest accomplishments were in

A scene from the construction of the Panama Canal

conservation. He loved the outdoors, and he was concerned that human development would take over natural areas. So he set aside nearly 200 million acres for national parks and wildlife refuges. Without Teddy Roosevelt, we might not be able to visit the Grand Canyon or camp in Glacier National Park in Montana. And some say that without Leon Czolgosz, we wouldn't have these parks either.

Roosevelt's presidency ended in 1909, and he set out for a 10-month African safari. When he returned, he discovered he didn't like what the current president, Howard Taft, was doing. So he decided to run for president again in 1912. The Republican Party didn't nominate him, so he created his own party, the Progressive Party, nicknamed the "Bull Moose" Party.

Why Bull Moose? Here's an interesting story: After McKinley's assassination, a man named John Schrank had a dream. In his dream the ghost of President McKinley appeared. The ghost pointed to a picture of Teddy Roosevelt and said, "This is my murderer. Avenge my death." So, in 1912, Schrank followed Roosevelt on the campaign trail. In Milwaukee, Wisconsin, Roosevelt was preparing to make a speech. He stepped out of a hotel, and Schrank shot him. The bullet passed through Roosevelt's fifty-page written speech and lodged in his chest. But Roosevelt didn't go to the doctor. He went on to give his 90-minute speech, saying that "It takes more than [one bullet] to kill a Bull Moose."

Roosevelt didn't win the election. He finished second, and Taft finished third. Roosevelt received the largest number of third-party votes in history. The presidency went to Democrat Woodrow Wilson. Wilson actually adopted many of Roosevelt's progressive ideas. He continued antitrust ideas and labor reform. Progressive reforms continued under another Roosevelt, Teddy's fifth cousin Franklin Delano Roosevelt, who became president in 1933.

William McKinley's presidency was overshadowed by Teddy Roosevelt. Many historians consider Roosevelt one of the top five presidents in history, but McKinley has largely been forgotten. Even the nation's tallest mountain, once called Mount McKinley, has had its previous name, Denali, restored. But remember that he was popular in his time. So, what might have happened if Leon Czolgosz hadn't killed McKinley? What would the nation have been like?

McKinley probably would not have set aside land for national parks and forests. McKinley wasn't moved by nature in the way Roosevelt was. Swaths of that land probably would have been mined, trees would've been chopped down, and houses and businesses would've been built. If you wanted to see the Grand Canyon, you might have had to trespass on private property for a glimpse.

And McKinley most certainly wouldn't have supported antitrust laws. Historians suggest large monopolies would have continued under his presidency. They say the gap between rich and poor would have continued to widen. Those things are perhaps true. But Leon Czolgosz wasn't the only one upset about the rich getting richer and the poor getting poorer. Many Americans were seeking change without violence. The public probably would have called for reforms like the trust-busting, even without Teddy Roosevelt.

Theodore Roosevelt often gets the credit for strengthening the nation's military, but McKinley had already set the idea in motion. Under McKinley the United States grew into an empire and a world power, so a strong military was in McKinley's sights. And the Panama Canal was within his sights too. The French were already starting to build it, and they had asked for America's help. The Senate would have voted to support it, no matter who was president.

Some people even say Czolgosz's crime cleared the way for progressive reform. Maybe these reforms would have happened without murder, maybe they would've come much later or in different forms, or maybe not at all. But history can't be rewritten. The facts remain. In 1901 a disgruntled man with a hidden gun killed our president. Those bullets rang in the end of the old and the beginning of the new. The 20th century dawned, and with it a fiery, young, new president who made lasting changes. Today we can still hear the echo of Leon Czolgosz's gunshots.

TIMELINE >>>>>>>>>>>>>>>>>>>>>>>>>>

Jan. 29, 1843: William McKinley is born in Niles, Ohio

Sept. 17, 1862: McKinley performs heroic act of bringing rations to soldiers during the Battle of Antietam

May 5, 1873: Leon Czolgosz is born in Alpena, Michigan, to Polish immigrant parents

1893: An economic crash hits the nation; Leon Czolgosz takes part in a workers' strike and is fired

Nov. 3, 1896: Republican William McKinley wins the presidential election

March 4, 1897: McKinley is sworn in as the nation's 25th president

1898: Leon Czolgosz quits his job and moves in with his family; he becomes interested in anarchy

Feb. 15, 1898: USS *Maine* explodes in Havana Harbor

April 25, 1898: War is formally declared between the United States and Spain

Dec. 10, 1898: The Spanish-American War ends with the signing of the Treaty of Paris between the U.S. and Spain

July 29, 1900: Italy's King Umberto I is assassinated

Nov. 6, 1900: William McKinley is elected to serve a second term as president

May 1, 1901: The World's Fair — called the Pan-American Exposition — opens in Buffalo

May 6, 1901: Czolgosz hears Emma Goldman speak

Aug. 31, 1901: Czolgosz goes to Buffalo, New York, and rents a room

Sept. 4, 1901: President McKinley arrives in Buffalo

Sept. 5, 1901: Czolgosz attends President McKinley's speech

Sept. 6, 1901: Czolgosz shoots President McKinley twice — once in the chest and once in the abdomen

Sept. 14, 1901: President McKinley dies of his wounds; Theodore Roosevelt takes the oath of office and becomes president

Sept. 23, 1901: Czolgosz goes on trial for the murder of William McKinley; Czolgosz is convicted and sentenced to death

Oct. 29, 1901: Leon Czolgosz is executed by electric chair

Oct. 14, 1912: Theodore Roosevelt is shot while on the campaign trail but is not seriously injured

1914: The Panama Canal is completed

1919: Anarchist Emma Goldman is deported to Russia

John F. Kennedy and his wife, Jacqueline, during the 1960 presidential campaign

PART IV

PRESIDENT KENNEDY'S KILLER
AND THE AMERICA HE LEFT BEHIND
THE ASSASSIN, THE CRIME, AND
THE END OF A HOPEFUL VISION
IN CHAOTIC TIMES

President John F. Kennedy

CHAPTER 16
A PROMISING PRESIDENT

It's a storied name, Kennedy. It's a name that rings of an exciting time of change in American history and of incredible, unbelievable tragedy. It's a name that recalls a famous family that in many ways was the closest the United States ever came to having royalty. The Kennedys were a wealthy clan with many children, some of whom became powerful Americans. One of them became president of the United States.

Famous and glamorous and seen as heroic, the Kennedys captured the country's imagination. And when he became president, John F. Kennedy asked his fellow Americans to use their imaginations, challenging them to "ask not what your country can do for you, but what you can do for your country."

Young, witty, and handsome, John F. Kennedy was a new kind of president for the time, and according to some historians, he was an effective and promising president — possibly a great one.

He was the second son of Rosemary Fitzgerald and Joseph P. Kennedy, a pair who met at the beginning of the 20th century in Maine. Joe, a Harvard University graduate, was at age 25 the youngest bank president in the world. From the day she was born, Rosemary Fitzgerald lived a fairy-tale life of riches and respect in Boston. Rosemary's father, nicknamed "Honey" Fitzgerald, served as a member of Congress for three terms, then worked as a newspaper publisher before running successfully for mayor of Boston. The family was so rich and powerful, in fact, that they at first didn't want Rosemary to get all that comfy with the young banker, Joseph Kennedy. They didn't think he was good enough for their daughter.

But Joe and Rosemary didn't care. Their two families could only stand by and watch as the two fell in love and married in 1914. Their family began growing shortly afterward, starting with the birth of Joseph Jr. and, two years later, of John Fitzgerald. He was born May 29, 1917, in an upstairs bedroom of a two-and-a-half story house in Boston. Around the time of John's birth, his father left banking and moved into the steel industry, then into stockbroking. He made millions of dollars. The family grew as his fortunes did, and eventually the Kennedys had nine children.

Growing up, John Fitzgerald Kennedy was known as "Jack." Like his mother, he enjoyed many of the spoils that come with a rich upbringing. There were maids, nurses, and a big family. Kennedy would later describe it as "an easy, prosperous life."

He liked to compete, and he competed with nobody more than his older brother, Joseph Jr. The two would fight frequently, with Jack frustrated by his older brother's athletic edge. They once played a game of "chicken" on their bikes, riding them at full speed toward

Joseph and Rose Kennedy had nine children, eight of whom are pictured here. John Kennedy stands third from the right, alongside his parents.

the other to see who would turn away first. They collided head-on. Joe was unhurt, John's injuries required 28 stitches.

Like his older brother, John Kennedy in 1936 attended Harvard University. In 1937, President Franklin Roosevelt appointed Joseph Kennedy Sr. ambassador to Great Britain, a prestigious and important role.

For John, his famous family became a part of life to deal with, and he did so with dignity. During college, he would occasionally see plays in which the Kennedys were the subject of jokes. John laughed along with the audiences. Despite being somebody raised with riches, Kennedy was not aloof or unkind.

As he matured, he became somebody who working people liked, admired, and trusted. He learned compassion early in life. His younger sister, Rosemary, was born with mental disabilities. In those times, it was common to send such children to institutions, but

Joseph and Rosemary Kennedy tried for years to keep her at home. They also insisted that Rosemary's brothers and sisters treat her as an equal, which they all did.

Not many saw John Kennedy's compassion first-hand. But a lot of Americans would read about his courage. Kennedy entered the U.S. Navy in October of 1941, just a few months before the United States was plunged into World War II. Despite severe health problems that included a constantly painful back, Kennedy asked for active duty instead of the office jobs he was first given. He was put in charge of a PT (patrol-torpedo) boat. It was one of the most dangerous jobs in military service. When his father arranged to have him made a trainer instead of a fighter, John Kennedy was furious. He argued with the military officials until they agreed to let him go into combat zones.

Kennedy's bravery showed itself during the war. His boat, PT-109, was rammed and split in half by a Japanese destroyer. Kennedy and the survivors of the crash were sent into the ocean. He and five other members first clung to the hull of the boat. Kennedy and two others swam out and helped five more crew members back to the floating wreckage. Two men died and were never found.

After nine hours of holding onto the boat, Kennedy and the other survivors made their way to a small island in the distance. Swimming on his stomach, Kennedy towed one of his injured crewmen by clenching the lifejacket ties in his teeth while the crewman floated behind. It was a five-hour swim. Once they made the island, Kennedy decided to try to swim out and flag down a boat. Most had believed the crew died in the sinking of PT-109. After seven days, ravaged by thirst and hunger, the survivors were rescued. The dramatic story of

Kennedy receives a medal for his service during his Navy years.

PT-109 and Kennedy's care for his men raised spirits back home. It was exactly the kind of story Americans needed to hear in wartime.

Kennedy's status as an American hero played well after the war. Two years into peacctime, he entered politics and ran for the U.S. House of Representatives. He hadn't always been interested in politics. His family, in fact, had been counting on his older brother,

Joe, to run for office. Strong, outgoing, and handsome, Joe Kennedy seemed destined to be a politician after his military service. During World War II, he flew bombers over Europe and completed 25 successful missions. But during a high-risk mission on August 12, 1944, his plane exploded. Joe Kennedy and another pilot were killed. John Kennedy had lost his older brother and role model.

After the war Kennedy was looking at two career choices — law and journalism. Neither possibility thrilled him. He saw being a lawyer as too boring compared to actually making laws to help the country. He saw journalism as being too much an observer, not a participant, in important events.

He saw in politics, however, an opportunity to make a difference, to strengthen and defend his country. Helped in large part by his father's money, Kennedy entered the Congressional race in Massachusetts at age 29. He easily won a seat in the House of Representatives in 1946.

Kennedy and Lyndon B. Johnson campaign in Austin, Texas.

Kennedy served three terms before running for and winning a seat in the U.S. Senate. In his run for Senate, he brought in his younger brother Robert to run the campaign. Robert, known as "Bobby," was working as a lawyer for the U.S. Department of Justice.

In 1953, about a year after he was elected to the

Senate, Kennedy married Jacqueline Bouvier. The two had met in 1951 at a dinner party. They had a lot in common. Most obviously, both were young, attractive members of wealthy families.

In the time Kennedy was in Congress, lawmakers were greatly concerned about communism and Soviet Russia's intent on world domination. He would deal with those issues more than once during his presidency.

As his time in Congress went on, Kennedy's ambition grew. His six years in the Senate saw him emerge as a leader on foreign affairs. He had proven himself an expert on foreign policy, and he did so as a fresh young voice in a government run mostly by old men. As early as 1956, when he sought unsuccessfully to be the vice-presidential nominee for the Democrats, his name was mentioned as a promising candidate for president. Kennedy felt he could do more as president than as senator, and he announced in January 1960 that he would run.

The election pitted him against Republican Richard Nixon. In some ways, it was a battle of styles. Television was replacing radio as a source for news, and Kennedy's youth, good looks, and comfort on TV gave him an advantage. Nixon often looked nervous and uncomfortable on TV. (Their debates have been used as examples of how important it became to look good on television.) But Nixon had been vice president under Dwight Eisenhower, and earlier he had served with distinction in noncombat roles during World War II.

The election race was close and hard-fought. Winning by the slightest margin, John F. Kennedy became 35th president of the United States. He was the youngest man ever elected to the office. He also represented the hopes and dreams of an entire country.

Lee Harvey Oswald

CHAPTER 17
THE MAKING OF A KILLER

Lee Harvey Oswald moved through life confused and angry. He saw himself as a world-class soldier, a great thinker, and a political expert. Reality kept showing otherwise. His high opinion of himself was simply not shared by many.

By the time he cleared a spot on the sixth floor of the brick building where he worked in Dallas and pointed his rifle at the back of John F. Kennedy's head, he was not doing well in life. He was, in fact, a near-broke father of two children with a crumbling marriage and low-paying job that involved moving cardboard boxes of textbooks.

Likely, Oswald did what he did because, like other assassins before and after him, he had a twisted desire to be as famous as the person he killed. He achieved world fame, but as nothing but a killer who denied the world a popular, effective leader.

If Oswald had some political reason to murder his president — any reason — he took it to the grave. He never spoke of hating or even disliking the president, and he loved to speak his mind. As a teen Oswald spoke of disliking then-president Dwight D. Eisenhower, but as an adult Oswald rarely if ever spoke ill of John F. Kennedy. At the time he shot Kennedy, Oswald's political passions were in support of Communist-controlled Cuba, the island country that caused President Kennedy so much grief.

Oswald was born into a troubled family. His father died a few months before Lee's birth in New Orleans, Louisiana, in 1939. Oswald had a childhood swamped by change after change. His mother struggled to find good work and pay the bills. Much of Oswald's early childhood was spent either with an aunt or, once he was 3 years old, with his brothers at a home for orphans and children with one parent. It was called the Bethlehem Children's Home.

After his mother married again in the 1940s, Lee's older brothers attended military school. But Lee stayed home and found himself watching an increasingly unhappy marriage. His mother and stepfather fought frequently and eventually divorced.

Oswald as a child

His difficult family life continued as he moved from city to city while his mother pursued work. By the time Lee moved to Fort Worth, Texas, the family had moved 16 times. Still, Lee at first did well in most subjects at school. He attended classes quietly and paid attention. But by age 13, living in New York with his mother, he began having problems. Skipping school was one of them. A Youth

Court judge placed him in a home for boys, where one social worker saw him as seriously withdrawn and troubled.

The social worker wrote of him: "It seems fairly clear that he has detached himself from the world around him because no one in it ever met any of his needs for love."

As a high school student in the 1950s, Oswald became fascinated with communism , a system of government at odds with American ideals of freedom. Communism was growing among eastern European nations, in Southeast Asia, and elsewhere. Its leaders sought world control, clearly seen as a threat to the way of life in the United States.

The world had entered a period called the Cold War. That was the term applied to years of tension between the United States and the Soviet Union (and other communist-controlled or communist-leaning countries) after World War II. Oswald would go on to embrace communism at a time when the U.S. population — including U.S. Senator John F. Kennedy — grew increasingly nervous about its spread. American communists, in fact, were required to register with the government.

Driving Oswald's deep attraction to communism may have been its principle that the workers of the world were being pushed around by the rich and powerful. Oswald likely felt he had been pushed around too much, by everybody from the Youth Court judge to kids who liked to

Oswald during his Marines stint

beat him up. It's also possible that, given his family situation and his inability to make friends, he simply sought a group to which he could belong.

Oswald dropped out of high school and at age 17 enlisted in the U.S. Marines, serving for three years in both the United States and Japan. He showed more problem behavior in the Marines. First he accidentally shot himself with an unregistered handgun. Later he assaulted a superior officer. That led to his serving 45 days in military jail.

While in the Marines, he read books on Marxism and communism and dreamed of someday moving to Russia. Oswald finally faked a hardship case to get an early discharge. He claimed he had to take care of his mother. Soon after he was released, however, he traveled to Moscow, the capital of the Soviet Union and the power center of communism. Once there, he took steps to become a Soviet citizen, but he was denied. Oswald went so far as visiting the U.S. Embassy in Moscow to renounce his American citizenship. He even attempted suicide rather than return to the U.S.

His devotion to communism, however, wasn't very sophisticated. An American Embassy official asked him not only about why he wanted to stay in the Soviet Union but about communism itself. Oswald, it turned out, didn't know all that much about it. That official later said Oswald had a "flaky" enthusiasm and "didn't have the slightest idea what this country (the Soviet Union) was all about."

In the meeting at the embassy, Oswald made a vague threat. He said he could offer the Soviets information he had as the result of his time in the Marines. The American official quickly notified the U.S. government about what Oswald said. He also told the Moscow chief of United Press International news service to seek Oswald out for a news story.

Oswald agreed to be interviewed by an American journalist. In early November 1959, American newspapers including the *New York Times* carried the bizarre story of the American Marine who wanted to become a Soviet citizen. So, for a while, Oswald was getting attention and recognition. He defended his anti-American views in a letter to his brother, writing at one point: "In the event of war I would kill any American who put a uniform on in defense of the American government — any American."

While keeping him under close watch in case he was an American spy, the Soviets allowed Oswald to stay in the country for at least a year. They assigned him a factory job in a town 400 miles from Moscow. Once he got a full taste of Russian work life, though, Oswald began to have second thoughts. As he wrote in a diary (his spelling corrected here), "I am starting to reconsider my desire about staying. The work is drab, the money I get has nowhere to be spent. No nightclubs or bowling alleys, no places of recreation except the trade union dances. I have had enough."

He was also shocked to discover the Soviet system was nothing like the ideal society he thought it would be. Just like the American economy, communism had its share of rich people and poor people. It was not a system where everyone was treated equally and fairly. In February 1961 he began asking for his American passport back and stated his desire to return to the United States.

While he awaited an answer, Oswald fell in love with a Russian woman, Marina Prusakova. The two met at a dance. They married in April 1961, later having a daughter, whom they named June. Oswald received permission to return to the U.S. In June 1962, the family left Russia and arrived in Fort Worth, Texas, where Oswald's brother and mother lived. Oswald's first words to his brother upon getting off the plane were: "No reporters?"

The two lived with Oswald's family for a while, and in the summer of 1962, Oswald found work at a welding company. In the fall, however, he told Marina and friends he had been fired and needed to move to Dallas to find more work. There he found a job in a printing house and rented a small, dirty apartment for his family.

Oswald was at that time subscribing to Communist newspapers and magazines. At one point, he sought to join the Socialist Workers Party.

On March 12, 1963, Oswald used a fake name to purchase two guns by mail — a handgun and a World War II model Italian rifle with a scope. Both guns would be used on November 22, 1963. He told Marina they were for hunting someday. She was mad he bothered with this expense when the family was low on food.

By this time, Oswald was writing a journal that indicated he was upset with the Communist Party of the United States as well as the Soviets. In his writings, he called for a new party that would "bring about the final destruction" of American society.

The communist revolt in Cuba captured Oswald's attention. In March 1963, he began writing to a group called Fair Play for Cuba Committee, which was critical of Kennedy's treatment of Cuba. Oswald stood on a busy street corner in Dallas and passed out pro-Cuba pamphlets. The materials criticized the U.S. for not welcoming Cuba's move toward communism under its new leader, Fidel Castro.

Oswald had other plans to draw attention to himself. He asked

Oswald asked his wife to photograph him as he posed with his guns.

his wife to take a photo of him holding his new rifle in one hand and two Marxist newspapers, *The Worker* and *The Militant,* in the other. This photo also shows him holstering a pistol. He told his wife he was going to send the photo to *The Militant* to show he was "ready for anything."

Oswald did just that. He sent the photo to *The Militant.* The woman who handled the newspaper's subscriptions saw the picture of a "kooky" looking guy holding a gun and the two papers. She

Lee Oswald with his wife, Marina, and their infant daughter in Russia in 1962

thought it quite odd that the two newspapers represented opposite viewpoints on political matters. The entire point of the photo, she thought, was "really dumb and totally naive."

A few weeks after the guns arrived in the mail, Oswald lost his job at the printing company. At some point, Oswald's view of himself switched to something far more sinister than a socialist. He saw himself as an assassin, and his first target was a former U.S. Army general named Edwin Walker.

Walker was a leader in the John Birch Society, a national group formed in 1958. The group was considered ultra-conservative and anti-communist. Walker was a champion to those who feared both communism and equal rights for African Americans. Walker had become a controversial figure and had even defended the likes of George Lincoln Rockwell, head of the American Nazi Party.

Walker's return to Dallas had taken place on the same day Oswald told his family he needed to find work in that city. Oswald spent weeks watching Walker's home and taking photos. Then on April 10, 1963, he stood outside the home with a gun. Oswald spotted Walker through a window, aimed, and fired. Oswald fled immediately, stashing the gun at the scene.

He discovered by reading the newspapers the following day that his shot missed. Walker had survived the attack. Nobody traced the shooting to Oswald, not even when he returned to the scene the following day to retrieve the rifle.

Oswald soon moved with his wife and child to New Orleans. He made a minor name for himself again by handing out pro-Cuba materials on the streets and being interviewed on the radio about his support for the communists there. He took a job at a coffee company in New Orleans. At work he behaved like a loner and paid little attention to his duties. His wife was pregnant again and, at times, was afraid of Oswald's violent temper. She left him in New Orleans and moved to a Dallas suburb. Oswald attempted to get permission to visit Cuba, saying he would continue traveling to the Soviet Union. But neither country seemed eager to have him and denied his immediate requests.

Lee Harvey Oswald returned to Dallas in October 1963. He was living in a rented room and trying to reconcile with his wife. Marina, who would soon give birth to their second daughter, told him about a possible job. Marina said she had met a woman whose brother just found a job and could maybe help Oswald get one at the same place. Connections were made, and on October 16, 1963, Oswald began working at the Texas School Book Depository. Little more than a month later, he would aim his rifle through an open window on the building's sixth floor. He would kill the president from there.

Communist leaders Fidel Castro (left) of Cuba and Nikita Khrushchev of the Soviet Union

CHAPTER 18
A TIME OF DANGER

In his time as president, John F. Kennedy handled some of the most dangerous threats ever posed to the United States. Many historians now consider it safe to say he was the right leader at the right time. His leadership protected freedom and might have prevented nuclear war.

If things had gone wrong, we might not be here, comfortably reading about that point in history. Thousands if not millions of people might have died from nuclear strikes in a fight to the death with the Soviet Union. The environment Kennedy inherited as president was dangerously tense between the communists in Soviet Russia and the United States.

That tension and struggle, called the Cold War, began after World War II. The U.S., Great Britain, and the Soviet Union had been allies in defeating Hitler's Germany. But the allies did not agree on what should happen after their victory. The Soviets began installing and supporting communist governments in eastern

Europe. Communism took hold in countries such as Poland, Hungary, Romania, and Czechoslovakia.

Communism put the government's needs before people. It kept tight control over everything from a country's economy to religion to freedom to live wherever one chose. This went against American ideals of democracy and freedom, and the spread of communism to any country, near or far, was seen as a threat and something to be fought against and wiped out wherever possible.

Making matters more hostile was the development of nuclear weapons. Both the United States and the Soviet Union now had nuclear weapons — aimed at each other.

In 1961, Kennedy took charge of a plan started under the previous president. In 1959 the pro-U.S. government of Cuba had been overthrown by rebels loyal to Fidel Castro, who became Cuba's president. Castro's ties with the Soviet Union made the U.S. military and political leaders nervous. In response, the U.S. secretly trained more than 1,400 Cubans to invade the country. The hope was that the invasion would inspire other Cubans to overtake and kick out Castro and his Soviet-supported government.

President Kennedy's advisers from the military and the Central Intelligence Agency (CIA) told him it would go smoothly. They said the invasion would appear to be a Cuban uprising, nothing involving the United States. Kennedy hesitantly approved the plan. The invaders would use disguised U.S. planes and ships to launch their invasion at Cuba's Bay of Pigs.

The operation failed at every end. Paratroopers landed in the wrong places. Ships sank before hitting the shore. In the end, more than 100 of the invaders were killed, and more than 1,200

Captured U.S.-backed soldiers after the failed Bay of Pigs invasion

surrendered. Some advisers pressured Kennedy to send U.S. troops into the mess, but he refused. The president was furious and blamed the CIA and the military advisers — the Joint Chiefs of Staff — for misleading him about the plan.

From that point on, the president would always weigh the opinion of military leaders with some distrust. Eventually his guarded attitude about the opinions of military advisers served him well. It might've been what prevented the U.S. and the Soviet Union from bombing each other with nuclear weapons.

The Bay of Pigs certainly did not ease the relationship between the U.S. and Soviet Union. The head of the Soviet government, Nikita Khrushchev, continually boasted that communism was the superior form of government. He also accused the U.S. of wanting to start military conflicts.

The failure in Cuba weakened Kennedy's approach when it came to a showdown with the Soviets over Berlin. After World War II, Germany had been split into four zones, each controlled by one of the four Allied powers who defeated the Germans: the U.S., France, Great Britain, and the Soviet Union. Although Berlin was in the Soviets' occupation zone and under Communist control, it was also divided between east and west. The United States, France, and Britain controlled West Berlin, and the Soviets occupied East Berlin.

But Khrushchev called for an end to that deal in 1958. He insisted that the U.S., Britain, and France get out of Berlin so the Soviets could unite the city. The Soviet system had not been working well in East Berlin. More and more people were crossing over into West Berlin, embarrassing the Soviets and ruining their hopes of a strong Communist city. The U.S. refused to move out, protecting freedom in West Berlin.

President Kennedy with the mayor of West Berlin, Willy Brandt

This was the situation when Kennedy took office, and meetings between the old Communist Khrushchev and the young U.S. president did not go well. Khrushchev, loud and colorful but often insulting, had the upper hand in conversations. The stakes were high, and Kennedy was under frequent pressure to consider a war plan to save West Berlin. After the two met in Vienna, Khrushchev made matters worse by halting progress toward a ban on nuclear weapons testing.

In a televised address, Kennedy explained the situation to the American people. He told them that he wasn't going to let the Soviets take over West Berlin. He said, "We cannot and will not permit the communists to drive us out of Berlin, either gradually or by force . . . we will at all times be ready to talk, if talk will help. But we must also be ready to resist with force, if force is used upon us."

With both sides firm, the world watched to see who would make the next move. Less than a month after Kennedy's get-tough speech, East German forces threw up barriers that blocked access from East Berlin to West Berlin, eventually constructing a wall.

Realizing the U.S. would not back down, Khrushchev had decided upon this solution. It struck Kennedy that Khrushchev was no longer interested in taking over West Berlin. "This is his way out of a predicament," Kennedy said. "It's not a very nice solution, but a wall is a hell of a lot better than a war."

Compared to the Bay of Pigs, this was a win. After the wall was built, Kennedy helped cool a showdown between tanks aiming at each other from opposite sides of the wall. Talking directly to Khrushchev, Kennedy offered that if the Soviet Union pulled its tanks, the U.S. would as well.

Not a year later, the distrust between the U.S. and the Soviet Union boiled up again. Tensions led to what is known as the Cuban Missile Crisis — considered by some to be Kennedy's shining moment (or shining days) in the White House.

Because Khrushchev was worried that the U.S. was planning to overthrow Cuba, he decided to use Cuba as a nuclear missile base. In October 1962, Khrushchev began shipping missiles to Cuba, an island about 90 miles from Florida. The Soviets sent missiles that could carry nuclear weapons 1,000 miles into the U.S. They sent other missiles that could travel 2,000 miles.

It was Cold War thinking: The U.S. had missiles in Turkey and Italy, both near Soviet-controlled territory. So Khrushchev believed he should give Americans a taste of what it was like having nuclear weapons pointed at them from a short distance away. Kennedy wanted no such taste. He was determined to not let shipments of those missiles get through to the island country so near to the U.S.

But Soviet ships were heading for Cuba with parts to keep building missiles. The Soviets were deliberately provoking the U.S. to either act or stand by while nuclear weapons were assembled. Kennedy needed to figure out how to stop the shipments and the build-up in Cuba without sparking war.

To invade Cuba, as his military advisers pressed him to do, would be an act of war. Such an act surely could trigger a nuclear exchange with the Soviets. Kennedy sought advice for any possible peaceful way out, all while the Soviets insisted on their right to build the missiles for their own protection.

Kennedy decided an invasion had to be a last resort. He put U.S. Navy ships around Cuba to prevent Soviet ships from reaching it. If

A U.S. destroyer (at front) and Navy plane escort a Soviet freighter carrying missiles away from Cuba.

the move failed, air strikes and an invasion of Cuba would follow — as would a probable nuclear strike. Congressional leaders insisted that the blockade was a sign of weakness. They urged Kennedy to strike Cuba quickly.

On a Monday night, Americans heard from their president that Cuba was installing nuclear weapons and the missiles could hit Washington, D.C., or any other city in the American southeast. Kennedy said the U.S. could not tolerate this advance and would "quarantine" Cuba. The U.S. was blocking all offensive weapons from reaching the island. If the Soviet didn't stop the buildup, the U.S. would take action, Kennedy explained. If Cuba used any of the nuclear missiles already in place against the U.S., the U.S. would use nuclear missiles against the Soviet Union.

On October 25, 1962, a few Soviet ships began turning around. They were followed by more. Kennedy had once again kept his more aggressive advisers at bay while he tried to reason with Khrushchev. In what seemed the last minute, Khrushchev agreed to turn the missiles around and eliminate them from Cuba. In return, he was promised the U.S. would leave Cuba alone. As he had with Berlin, Kennedy found a way to not be persuaded by those who were itching for war.

Biographer Robert Dallek writes that Kennedy's greatest achievements as president "were his management of Soviet-American relations and his effectiveness in discouraging a U.S. military mindset that accepted the possibility — indeed, even likelihood — of a nuclear war with Moscow."

The world did not get to benefit from Kennedy's calm and thoughtful approach when it came to what would become America's longest war up to that point: the war in Vietnam. In this distant Asian country, communist-led North Vietnam was fighting against South Vietnam, which was backed by the United States. If South Vietnam fell to the communists, it was feared, neighboring countries would follow what was called a "domino effect."

Kennedy was familiar with the struggles in Vietnam, which until the 1950s had been under the control of France. He was uncertain about how the U.S. should respond to the push southward by the North Vietnamese. Again, his top aides all believed military action was a good idea. Secretary of State Dean Rusk and Defense Secretary Robert McNamara reported that the fall of South Vietnam would be "extremely dangerous."

By late 1963 South Vietnamese forces had been joined by

16,000 American military "advisers." The U.S. troops were there to advise and guide the South Vietnamese army. But the situation grew worse every day. The North Vietnamese kept striking. Reporters on the scene were doing stories that opposed the optimistic reports made by the Kennedy advisers.

South Vietnamese President Ngo Diem was losing the support of his people. Finally, Kennedy authorized a military removal of Diem, which resulted in Diem being assassinated. This was not the result Kennedy expected. He increasingly realized how chaotic this conflict could be, and he knew it needed to be addressed somehow.

Nearly every member of his national security and defense team called for U.S. troops to fight on behalf of South Vietnam before the country fell to communism. Kennedy's experience told him he needn't take his advisers' word as the final say. He believed communism was a threat to world security. But he also saw that this country was more than 8,000 miles away and that the South's army of 200,000 was not having any success. Was it worth sending young Americans to fight and die?

Kennedy had a lot to think about when his plane landed in Dallas in November 1963.

President Kennedy visited Tampa, Florida, before traveling to Texas in November 1963.

CHAPTER 19
A SHOCKING CRIME

In the early autumn of 1963, Kennedy had not said publicly that he would run for re-election the following year. But it seemed he was already campaigning. In September, the president visited nine states in less than one week. Although the visits were supposed to be about preserving natural resources, the speeches carried the feel of campaign stops. His talks eventually covered more exciting areas of concern such as world peace, education, and national security.

By November 1963, a year before the 1964 presidential election, Kennedy had begun serious campaign planning. His chances of winning were good. By the end of 1962, he was listed as the world leader admired most by Americans. In March 1963, polling showed most Americans believed he would be elected for a second term.

But he didn't want to take chances, and he knew he wasn't popular in at least two Southern states, Florida and Texas. He visited Florida on November 18, speaking to large groups in Tampa and Miami about the economy and foreign affairs.

On November 21 the president and his wife began what was to be a two-day, five-city tour of Texas. As far as Kennedy could tell, the Democratic party in Texas needed some repair. Opposing groups within the party were fighting each other — in some cases literally coming to blows. Kennedy believed a visit to the state could get Texas voters behind him and his Texan vice president, Lyndon Johnson. The rift in the party was especially strong in Dallas, so Kennedy made sure he would visit the city.

On the morning of November 22, Kennedy woke in Fort Worth. He soon spoke to a gathering of residents on the need for America's leadership in defense, space, and economic freedom. He later addressed the Fort Worth Chamber of Commerce. From that city, Kennedy took a 13-minute flight to Dallas, where he and Jackie were greeted by a cheering crowd offering their hands and a bouquet of red roses for Jackie. After shaking hands and talking with the crowd, the First Couple took the back seat of a convertible that would carry them on a parade through the streets of Dallas. In the seat in front of them were Texas Governor John Connally and his wife, Nellie.

A lunch speech by the president had been scheduled, and the president had agreed that they would drive through downtown Dallas. The drive would allow the president to wave from the back seat of the convertible to the hundreds of people gathered along the streets to catch a glimpse of him.

A few days earlier *The Dallas Morning News* had published a report on the route. The motorcade would travel first through downtown Dallas. The last segment would be a stretch in Dealey Plaza, a three-acre patch of grass and office buildings known as the "Front Door of Dallas." From there, the car would speed up and take the freeway to

The Kennedys arrive at the Dallas airport shortly before the president's assassination.

the president's destination, the Trade Mart, where he was scheduled to address an audience of about 2,000 people.

When the car turned onto Elm Street, it would pass below the Texas School Book Depository. Lee Harvey Oswald would be watching from above, rifle at his side.

That morning Oswald had been given a ride to work by a friend, who asked about the long bag Oswald was carrying. Oswald explained that it held curtain rods. Using the freight elevator or the stairs, Oswald arrived on the sixth floor of the building, stashed his

The Kennedys rode in a convertible with the governor of Texas, John Connally, and his wife, Nellie.

rifle nearby and began working — filling boxes with books.

For the next three hours, Oswald appeared to be just doing what he was supposed to do. Lunch hour approached, and while hundreds of people had crowded the downtown route, the Dealey Plaza section of the route — the final stretch — held fewer people. This was the stretch where the motorcade would finish up its slow, parade-like pace. Some people along the route were a mere six or seven feet from the president himself.

Oswald, finding himself alone on the sixth floor, eventually took his rifle and waited at a window for the moment he knew would come. When the motorcade turned on Elm Street and began traveling away from the building, Oswald aimed at the back of the president and began firing.

He fired three shots in a matter of seconds. The first shot missed, and the sound was mistaken by some in the president's motorcade as a motorcycle backfiring. Three and a half seconds later, the second shot was fired. This one hit Kennedy in the back. Connally too, was hit by the bullet and shouted, "They're going to kill us all." Connally's wife, Nellie, pulled him close to her, resting his head on her lap as she tried to protect him from the unknown line of fire.

Confused, Jackie Kennedy looked at her husband and the odd look on his face, as though he was suffering a headache. Just as the Secret Service called for the motorcade to speed up and head toward the hospital, a third shot pierced the back of the president's skull, tearing open his head. His body slumped and leaned into Jackie, who was now covered with her husband's blood.

The motorcade raced to Parkland Hospital, as news reports began explaining that the president had been shot, perhaps fatally. The situation was dire. While emergency room surgeons worked to save Governor Connally's life, the doctors were helpless against the terrible wounds Kennedy had suffered. Efforts to save him failed. The president was pronounced dead at 1 p.m.

Jackie Kennedy turned to the wounded president as the shots rang out.

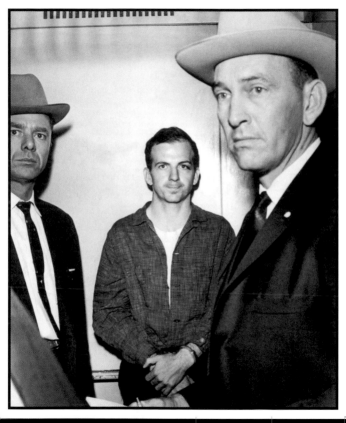

Lee Harvey Oswald in the custody of police after the assassination

CHAPTER 20
THE TROUBLING AFTERMATH

After firing three times, Lee Harvey Oswald dashed toward the back staircase. He hid the rifle between some boxes and ran down the stairway. On the way down, he encountered a police officer who was heading upstairs along with the Book Depository's manager. The two talked to Oswald briefly, with the manager explaining that Oswald belonged in the building as an employee. The officer continued up the stairs, and Oswald slipped into the pandemonium and confusion that overwhelmed the streets.

Oswald calmly walked seven blocks along Elm Street. He flagged down a city bus and, despite not being at a bus stop, the driver let him board. The bus had to slow down considerably because of the jammed traffic and panic in the area. Oswald got off the bus and hailed a taxi to take him to his rooming house, where he changed clothes, grabbed his pistol, and walked out.

Soon a Dallas police officer named J.D. Tippit noticed a man who sort of fit the physical description of the suspect given to police by witnesses. Tippit radioed for more specific descriptions while following the walking man slowly. Eventually Tippit pulled his squad car to the curb so he could ask the man, Oswald, some questions. Oswald approached the car and, through the open passenger window, talked with Tippit. When the officer got out of the car to talk further, Oswald pulled out his pistol and fired four shots at Tippit, killing him.

Then Oswald fled a few blocks, and as sirens wailed in response to the killing of Tippit, he ducked into a movie theater, sitting among the back rows. He wasn't there for long. Ten minutes later the lights in the theater glared on and police entered, capturing and arresting Oswald on suspicion of murdering Officer Tippit.

Police, meanwhile, had also found the rifle Oswald stashed in the book depository, as well as his bag and the empty shells. They would soon discover through serial number research that it was the gun purchased by Oswald through the mail. They found the same was true of the pistol used to kill officer Tippit.

The world watched Oswald as Dallas police allowed reporters to question him. He insisted he was innocent. He said upon being arrested that he wasn't sure what he was being charged with and denied any wrongdoing. Through reporters, Oswald asked for lawyers to step forward and help him, claiming he was "just a patsy."

"I didn't shoot anybody," he said at one point. "I haven't been told what I am here for." He also claimed that he was being held because he had lived in the Soviet Union.

On November 24, Americans watched their television sets to see

Jack Ruby emerged from the crowd and shot Oswald as officers escorted him through the lower level of the Dallas police station.

the memorial service for President Kennedy. Also that day Dallas police were moving Oswald from police headquarters to another location. The police had invited the press to film the transport, and as one network broadcast live on television, a man in a dark suit and hat moved forward, shoved a pistol at Oswald, and fired into his stomach. Oswald fell. The shooter, a nightclub owner named Jack Ruby, was arrested. Oswald was taken by ambulance to the same hospital where Kennedy had been taken.

Oswald died less than two hours after being shot, making no admission in the meantime of having done anything wrong. Investigations into his life and background found no clear reason why Oswald decided to assassinate Kennedy. Some people believe he wanted to prove himself to Soviet leaders as devoted to the Soviet cause. Whatever his motives were, they remain foggy even today.

The United States had lost a beloved president, and the free world lost a skilled leader. The question of why John Kennedy was killed would prove to be a difficult one to answer. Many people thought Oswald was part of a larger plan rather than one troubled man acting alone. But careful and thorough investigations have concluded that Oswald was alone in plotting and carrying out his crime.

With time, people began to wonder how the United States and the world might be different today had John Kennedy survived. Lyndon Johnson, who was sworn in as president soon after Kennedy's death, led the country in trying times. Historians now praise Johnson's work to promote civil rights and to assure fairness for African Americans and other minorities. But under Johnson, the country would plunge itself into war in Vietnam. The war and his handling of it cast a dark shadow over Johnson's presidency.

History presents an important question here. How would Kennedy have handled the Vietnam War had he lived? Might many lives have been saved? Might years of political unrest and division have been avoided?

These are painful questions, because 58,000 American lives and 2 million Vietnamese lives were lost in the Vietnam War. And in the end, many people say the war changed nothing.

By the time he was shot, Kennedy in his 1,000 days in office had earned a reputation as a true world leader, tough and thoughtful. He gained that reputation in the most difficult ways imaginable. More than once he made decisions that, if wrong, would have cost thousands of lives, perhaps millions.

So how would he have handled our country's approach to

Vietnam? During the few early years of the conflict, Kennedy did deal with it. His choices and thoughts in those years give a good idea of how to answer the question.

In the 1950s and early 1960s, not many Americans had heard of Vietnam, located more than 8,000 miles away in Southeast Asia. Until 1954 Vietnam and neighboring Laos and Cambodia had been under the control of France in what was called French Indochina.

That ended in 1954 when communist rebels led by Ho Chi Minh staged a four-month attack. They overpowered the French in the city of Dien Bien Phu in the northern part of Vietnam. The country was split into two nations, the communist-controlled North Vietnam and the independent, pro-U.S. country of South Vietnam.

Army units from North Vietnam, however, continued

Ho Chi Minh, leader of the Vietnamese communist revolutionaries

pressing into South Vietnam. Soldiers and leaders from the North saw their fight as one for Vietnamese independence. The U.S. perceived it as — or mistook it for — the spread of communism directed from China and Russia. From former president Dwight Eisenhower on down, officials had been terrified of more communist countries in the world. If South Vietnam fell, it was feared, the communists would control all of Southeast Asia. Before he left office, President Eisenhower sent military support and about 700 non-combat military personnel to Vietnam to help and train its army.

Fresh into his presidency in 1961, Kennedy had looked carefully at the Vietnam situation with one main goal — keeping American soldiers out of the conflict. He agreed to help South Vietnamese President Ngo Dinh Diem by giving him enough money to expand the South Vietnamese army to a total of 200,000 people.

Diem's government proved to be nothing but a headache to the United States. He behaved like a power-hungry tyrant — the worst possible example of democracy. Aside from his personal greed, he abused his own people. He violently suppressed the rights of the country's Buddhists, who were the country's majority. While supporting Diem with money and equipment, Kennedy urged Diem to change course. He told Diem that democracy in South Vietnam wasn't going to work out so well if most of its people detested him.

U.S. helicopters airlifted Vietnamese soldiers into battle against communist forces in 1965.

Diem constantly called for American help, knowing the U.S. was committed to keeping communism from spreading. In 1961 Kennedy again found himself one of the few people in his circle of advisers against going to war. His advisers told him the U.S. should send between 22,800 and 40,000 soldiers and take over the war from Diem.

Kennedy had not liked the idea of such an open-ended conflict. How could battles in distant jungles end well for the U.S.? In October 1961 he sent military officials and other advisers to visit Vietnam. He expected them to come back with the best possible plan. They returned with bad news: The U.S. couldn't act soon enough to prevent South Vietnam's fall to the communists. His advisers presented a plan calling for a "limited partnership" with the South Vietnamese in which 8,000 American troops would be sent to fight. Others who made the visit, including Kennedy's defense secretary, Robert McNamara, suggested sending 200,000 American soldiers.

While he and others knew South Vietnam could be lost to the Communists, Kennedy remained unconvinced about a military response. He questioned the idea of getting America involved in fighting in another country's civil war. What he told a newspaper reporter in 1961 turned out to be eerily accurate. Sending thousands of fighting troops would likely lead to demands for even more.

"They want a force of American troops," Kennedy said. "They say it's necessary in order to restore confidence and maintain morale. But . . . the troops will march in; the bands will play; the crowds will cheer; and in four days everyone will have forgotten. Then we will be told we have to send in more troops. It's like taking a drink. The effect wears off, and you have to take another."

Kennedy decided to provide more equipment and to more than double the 1,200 non-combat military advisers already there.

That term, "military advisers," had been an important one. It allowed Kennedy to help South Vietnam with American soldiers who could aid in battling the North Vietnamese but could not enter direct combat. It was a thin line, where helping ended and fighting began. Some people accused Kennedy of not being honest with the American people about military activity in the country.

He defended himself at a press conference, saying, "We have not sent combat troops in the generally understood sense of the word."

Kennedy continued to send these advisers — up to 16,000 by October 1963 — to help Diem. These advisers were no doubt seeing combat action in their aid of the South Vietnamese. More than a hundred American advisers were killed by the end of the year.

In 1963, Kennedy had been growing increasingly upset with Diem, whose rule was so corrupt and oppressive that it made communism a lot more attractive to the South Vietnamese. Diem had outlawed all political parties but his own and cracked down on any protests of his government. He even allowed for the killing of Buddhists who were peacefully demonstrating.

Kennedy had finally approved a secret plan for the military in South Vietnam to overthrow Diem. On November 2, 1963, Diem and his brother — a top adviser — were not only removed from office but assassinated. The result was chaos, and the North Vietnamese grew bolder. The U.S. now found itself further tangled up in a situation that troubled its leaders. At least some American leaders doubted the war was winnable.

Kennedy may have had enough. Even before Diem's overthrow,

Kennedy announced his desire to bring 1,000 troops home by the year's end. With advisers he had discussed the goal of having all American troops out by 1965.

Shortly before leaving for Dallas in November, Kennedy told Mike Forrestal, his advisor on Far East Affairs, to put together every option available in Vietnam, "including how we get out of there."

President Lyndon B. Johnson

Would Kennedy have removed the U.S. from Vietnam by 1965? Some actions he took in Vietnam give us clues. It's also important to look at the amount of caution Kennedy demonstrated not only in Vietnam, but throughout his presidency. His firm but careful responses had led to relatively peaceful results in conflicts with the Soviets. Of course, we can't know what Kennedy would have done about Vietnam. Many historians today believe he would have continued to back the South Vietnamese, just as his successor did.

In 1965, under Lyndon B. Johnson, the U.S. entered the war in Vietnam. Over the next 10 years, the war would cost many lives and tear apart those who supported the war and those who did not. And in the end, the North Vietnamese overtook South Vietnam.

Johnson faced an overwhelming push from every angle — military advisers, the media, and the public — to go into Vietnam and stop the spread of communism. Kennedy would have faced that as well. But Kennedy had something Johnson did not. He had experience dealing with military men who saw combat and war as a first option. Kennedy had a distrust for military leaders. It went back to his time in the Navy, and as president he'd watched top level military men talk seriously of nuclear war. Kennedy's caution clearly saved American lives during his presidency.

His experience standing up to military "experts" gave him a kind of confidence. He would have needed it if he chose to go against popular opinion over Vietnam. Johnson had no such reputation in foreign affairs. As vice president he usually sided with the advisers encouraging Kennedy to go to war.

During an interview with Walter Cronkite of CBS News, President Kennedy had expressed doubts about South Vietnam's ability to win the war and questioned the actions of President Ngo Dinh Diem.

Kennedy had been tested similarly before.

He had prevented the U.S. from getting involved in 1961 in Laos, another country in Southeast Asia. After France pulled out of Indochina, Laos and neighboring Cambodia were declared neutral countries. But a civil war soon broke out between the U.S.-supported government and the North Vietnamese-supported communist rebels. Kennedy had been encouraged by his advisers to send American troops, and some even suggested using nuclear weapons to prevent a communist takeover. Kennedy instead talked with Soviet Premier Nikita Khrushchev, and the two men agreed to a settlement. It was shaky, but it wasn't war.

Voters in 1964 would have had a clear choice. Kennedy would have been challenged by Barry Goldwater, an enthusiastic supporter of going to war in Vietnam. Given that choice and polling data from before the assassination, it seems the American people would probably have given Kennedy a second term. Nobody knows for sure. It's possible that Kennedy would have fulfilled a campaign promise of keeping the U.S. out of combat in Vietnam. Or he might have pursued the war but done so differently than Johnson did — for better or worse. Either way, the country might be a very different place today.

TIMELINE ›››››››››››››››››››››››››

May 29, 1917: John F. Kennedy is born in Boston to Joseph and Rose Kennedy; he will be raised in prosperity and comfort

Oct. 18, 1939: Lee Harvey Oswald is born in Louisiana; he will be raised off and on by a single mother struggling for work who frequently uprooted the family

October 1941: Kennedy joins the U.S. Navy shortly before the U.S. enters World War II

Dec. 7, 1941: Japan attacks the American forces at Pearl Harbor, Hawaii, triggering the U.S. entry into World War II

Aug. 1, 1943: Kennedy's torpedo patrol boat, the PT-109, is rammed by a Japanese destroyer; after saving the lives of his men, Kennedy is hailed as a hero

Nov. 5, 1946: After his first political campaign, Kennedy is elected to the U.S. House of Representatives from the 11th District in Massachusetts

Nov. 4, 1952: Kennedy is elected to the U.S. Senate

May 7, 1954: Following a military defeat against the communist North Vietnamese at Dien Bien Phu, France surrenders control of Indochina (Vietnam, Laos, and Cambodia)

October 1956: Oswald joins the U.S. Marines; his training includes marksmanship

Jan. 1, 1959: Fidel Castro leads the overthrow of a military dictatorship in Cuba and establishes communist rule in the island nation

October 1959: Having been interested in communism and Marxism for years, Oswald seeks to become a citizen of the Soviet Union

Jan. 2, 1960: Kennedy announces his candidacy for U.S. president

July 1960: Delegates at the 1960 Democratic Convention in Los Angeles nominate Kennedy as the party's presidential candidate, with Lyndon B. Johnson as the candidate for vice president

Sept. 21, 1960: Kennedy and Republican candidate Richard M. Nixon take part in the first televised presidential debate

Nov. 8, 1960: Kennedy wins a narrow victory over Nixon

Jan. 20, 1961: Kennedy is sworn in as president of the United States

May 11, 1961: Following a strategy started by President Eisenhower, Kennedy sends 500 U.S. soldiers and advisers to South Vietnam

June 1962: Oswald, with his wife and child, returns from the Soviet Union to the United States

October 1962: The U.S. discovers that Cuba is building a missile base; Kennedy, amid calls for an invasion, establishes a blockade to confront the oncoming Soviet ships delivering missiles

Nov. 22, 1963: Oswald shoots and kills President Kennedy in Dallas

Nov. 23, 1963: Oswald is shot and killed by nightclub owner Jack Ruby

GLOSSARY

abolitionist—a person who worked to end slavery before the Civil War

accomplice—a person who helps another person do something illegal or wrong

antiseptic—something that kills germs and prevents infection

armory—a place where weapons are stored

capitalism—economic system that allows people to freely create businesses and own as much property as they can afford

Cold War—a conflict between the United States and the Soviet Union; although there was no direct fighting, the conflict lasted from about 1947 to 1990

communism—system in which goods and property are owned by the government and shared in common; communist rulers limit personal freedoms to achieve their goals

conspirator—a person who is involved in a secret, illegal plan

corruption—willingness to do things that are wrong or illegal to get money, favors, or power

customs—the government department or checkpoint where imported goods are screened and duties on goods are collected

depository—a place where items are stored for safekeeping

empire—a group of countries or lands under one government or ruler

inauguration—formal ceremony to swear a person into political office

Marxist—person who believes in the theories of Karl Marx (considered the father of communism), who wrote that the struggles between rich and poor would be eliminated if there were no classes

monopoly—situation in which there is only one supplier of a good or service, and therefore that supplier can control the price and the market

nomination—choosing someone as a candidate for political office

secession—withdrawal or separation from a country or group, often to form another country or group

smuggle—to take something in or out of a place secretly or illegally

socialism—an economic system in which the goods made by factories, businesses, and farms are controlled by the government

strike—the refusal to work because of a disagreement with the employer over wages or working conditions

tyrant—someone who rules other people in a cruel or unjust way

SOURCE NOTES

Page 4, line 7: Steers, Edward Jr. *Blood on the Moon: The Assassination of Abraham Lincoln.* Lexington, Ky.: The University Press of Kentucky, 2001, p. 91.

Page 7, line 8: Holzer, Harold, Ed. *President Lincoln Assassinated!! The Firsthand Story of the Murder, Manhunt, Trial, and Mourning.* New York: Penguin Random House, 2014, p. 6.

Page 7, line 13: Booth, John Wilkes. *Right or Wrong, God Judge Me: The Writings of John Wilkes Booth.* Rhodehamel, John and Louise Taper, Eds. Urbana, Ill.: University of Illinois Press, 1997, p. 55.

Page 15, line 5: Holzer, Harold. "What if Abraham Lincoln Had Lived?" *CNN Politics. October 6, 2015.* http://www.cnn.com/2016/10/06/politics/had-abraham-lincoln-lived-counterfactual/index.html

Page 15, line 15: Carpenter, Francis Bicknell. *Six Months at the White House with Abraham Lincoln.* New York: Hurd and Houghton, 1866.; reprinted by Applewood Books in Bedford, Mass., pp 30-31.

Page 33, line 6: Axelrod, Alan. *Lincoln's Last Night: Abraham Lincoln, John Wilkes Booth, and the Last 36 Hours Before the Assassination.* New York: Penguin Group, 2005, p. 90.

Page 37. line 3: *Right or Wrong, God Judge Me: The Writings of John Wilkes Booth*, p. 154.

Page 38, line 1: *Blood on the Moon: The Assassination of Abraham Lincoln*, p. 204.

Page 42, line 17: Guelzo, Allen. "What if Abraham Lincoln Had Lived?" *The Washington Post.* 13 April 2015. October 2017. https://www.washingtonpost.com/posteverything/wp/2015/04/13/what-if-abraham-lincoln-had-lived/

Page 43, line 3: "What if Abraham Lincoln Had Lived?"

Page 57, line 7: Millard, Candice. *Destiny of the Republic: A Tale of Madness, Medicine and the Murder of a President.* New York: Doubleday, 2011, p.46.

Page 66, line 14: Ibid, p. 107.

Page 76, line 16: Ibid: p. 109.

Page 77, line 2: Ibid: p. 109.

Page 80, line 1: "Murder of a President." Narr. Michael Murphy. *American Experience.* PBS Television. 2 Feb. 2016.

Page 92, line 19: Hayes, H. G. and C. J. *A Complete History of the Life and Trial of Charles Guiteau, Assassin of President Garfield.* Philadelphia: Hubbard Bros. Publishers, 1882, p. 271.

Page 94, line 22: Ibid, p. 276.

Page: 94, line 25: Ibid, p. 276

Page: 95: *Destiny of the Republic: A Tale of Madness, Medicine and the Murder of a President*, p. 146.

Page 102, line 9: McKinley, William. *President McKinley's Last Speech.* New York: Henry Malkan, 1901.

Page 108, line 3: Miller, Scott. *The President and the Assassin: McKinley, Terror, and Empire at the Dawn of the American Century.* New York: Random House, 2011, p. 109.

Page 128, line 8: Ibid., p. 283.

Page 129, line 2: Ibid., p. 297.

Page 129, line 19: *President McKinley's Last Speech.*

Page 131, line 25: *The President and the Assassin: McKinley, Terror, and Empire at the Dawn of the American Century, p. 301.*

Page 132, line 2: Rauchway, Eric. *Murdering McKinley: The Making of Theodore Roosevelt's America.* New York: Farrar, Straus, and Giroux, 2003, p. 3.

Page 132, line 5: *The President and the Assassin: McKinley, Terror, and Empire at the Dawn of the American Century, p. 302.*

Page 133, line 4: *Murdering McKinley: The Making of Theodore Roosevelt's America, p. 19.*

Page 135, line 7: Vowell, Sarah. *Assassination Vacation.* New York: Simon & Schuster, 2005, p. 227.

Page 138, line 1: *The President and the Assassin: McKinley, Terror, and Empire at the Dawn of the American Century, p. 328.*

Page 138, line 5: Ibid, p. 330.

Page 142, line 1: "Who Shot T.R.?" National Park Service. 20 April 2017. October 2017.https://www.nps.gov/thrb/learn/historyculture/whoshottr.htm

Page 142, line 7: Ibid.

Page 162, line 3: Bugliosi, Vincent. *Reclaiming History: The Assassination of President John F. Kennedy.* New York: W.W. Norton & Company, Inc., 2007, p. 639.

Page 171, line 21: Dallek, Robert. *An Unfinished Life. John F. Kennedy 1917-1963.* New York: Black Bay Books/Little Brown and Company, 2003, p. 426.

Page 181, line 4: *Reclaiming History: The Assassination of President John F. Kennedy,* pp. 39-40.

Page 189, line 22: *An Unfinished Life. John F. Kennedy 1917-1963, p. 450.*

Page 190, line 8: Ibid, p. 458.

Page 191, line 10: Ibid, p. 686.

SELECT BIBLIOGRAPHY

PART I

Axelrod, Alan. *Lincoln's Last Night: Abraham Lincoln, John Wilkes Booth, and the Last 36 Hours Before the Assassination.* New York: Penguin Group, 2005.

Booth, John Wilkes. *Right or Wrong, God Judge Me: The Writings of John Wilkes Booth.* Rhodehamel, John and Louise Taper, Eds. Urbana, Ill.: University of Illinois Press, 1997.

Carpenter, Francis Bicknell. *Six Months at the White House with Abraham Lincoln.* New York: Hurd and Houghton, 1866.; reprinted by Applewood Books in Bedford, Mass.

Clarke, James W. *American Assassins: The Darker Side of Politics.* Princeton, N.J.: Princeton University Press, 1982.

Guelzo, Allen. "What if Abraham Lincoln Had Lived?" *The Washington Post.* 13 April 2015. October 2017. https://www.washingtonpost.com/posteverything/wp/2015/04/13/what-if-abraham-lincoln-had-lived/

Hodes, Martha. *Mourning Lincoln.* New Haven, Conn.: Yale University Press, 2015.

Holzer, Harold, Ed. *President Lincoln Assassinated!! The Firsthand Story of the Murder, Manhunt, Trial, and Mourning.* New York: Penguin Random House, 2014.

Kauffman, Michael W. *American Brutus: John Wilkes Booth and the Lincoln Conspiracies.* New York: Random House, 2004.

Leonard, Elizabeth. *Lincoln's Avengers: Justice, Revenge, and Reunion After the Civil War.* New York: W.W. Norton & Company, 2004.

Lindop, Edmund. *Assassinations that Shook America.* New York: Franklin Watts, 1992.

Steers, Edward Jr. *Blood on the Moon: The Assassination of Abraham Lincoln.* Lexington, Ky.: The University Press of Kentucky, 2001.

Swanson, James L. and Weinberg, Daniel R. *Lincoln's Assassins: Their Trial and Execution.* Santa Fe, N.M.: Arena Editions, 2001.

"What if Abraham Lincoln Had Lived?" *CNN Politics.* 6 October 2015. October 2017. http://www.cnn.com/2016/10/06/politics/had-abraham-lincoln-lived-counterfactual/index.html

PART II

Hayes, H. G. and C. J. *A Complete History of the Life and Trial of Charles Guiteau, Assassin of President Garfield.* Philadelphia: Hubbard Bros. Publishers, 1882.

Millard, Candice. *Destiny of the Republic: A Tale of Madness, Medicine and the Murder of a President.* New York: Doubleday, 2011.

"Murder of a President." Narr. Michael Murphy. *American Experience.* PBS Television. 2 Feb. 2016.

Ridings Jr., William J. and Stuart B. McIver. *Rating the Presidents.* New York: Kensington Publishing Corp., 2000.

Rutkow, Ira. *James A. Garfield. The American President Series.* New York: Times Books, 2006.

PART III

Clarke, James W. *American Assassins: The Darker Side of Politics.* Princeton, N.J.: Princeton University Press, 1982.

Creighton, Margaret. *The Electrifying Rise and Fall of Rainbow City: Spectacle and Assassination at the 1901 World's Fair.* New York: W.W. Norton & Company, 2016.

Halstead, Murat. *The Illustrious Life of William McKinley, Our Martyred President.* Chicago: Murat Halstead, 1901.

Lindop, Edmund. *Assassinations that Shook America.* New York: Franklin Watts, 1992.

McKinley, William. *President McKinley's Last Speech.* New York: Henry Malkan, 1901.

Miller, Scott. *The President and the Assassin: McKinley, Terror, and Empire at the Dawn of the American Century.* New York: Random House, 2011.

Rauchway, Eric. *Murdering McKinley: The Making of Theodore Roosevelt's America.* New York: Farrar, Straus, and Giroux, 2003.

Rove, Karl. *The Triumph of William McKinley: Why the Election of 1896 Still Matters.* New York: Simon & Schuster, 2015.

Vowell, Sarah. *Assassination Vacation.* New York: Simon & Schuster, 2005.

Williams, R. Hal. *Realigning America: McKinley, Bryan, and the Remarkable Election of 1896.* Lawrence, KS: University Press of Kansas, 2010.

"Who Shot T.R.?" National Park Service. 20 April 2017. October 2017.https:// www.nps.gov/thrb/learn/historyculture/whoshottr.htm

PART IV

Bugliosi, Vincent. *Reclaiming History: The Assassination of President John F. Kennedy.* New York: W.W. Norton & Company, Inc., 2007.

Blight, James G., Lang, Janet M., and Welch, David A. *Vietnam if Kennedy Had Lived: Virtual JFK.* Lanham, Md.: Rowman and Littlefield Publishers, 2009.

Caro, Robert. *The Passage of Power.* New York: Vintage Books, 2013.

Dallek, Robert. "JFK's Second Term." *The Atlantic.* June 2003.

Dallek, Robert. *An Unfinished Life. John F. Kennedy 1917-1963.* New York: Black Bay Books/ Little Brown and Company, 2003.

Greenfield, Jeff. *If Kennedy Lived: The First and Second Terms of President John F. Kennedy: An Alternate History.* New York: G.P. Putnam's Sons, 2013.

Ridings Jr., William J. and Stuart B. McIver. *Rating the Presidents.* New York: Kensington Publishing Corp., 2000.

INDEX

abolitionists, 17, 19, 22
African Americans, 15, 22, 23, 36, 39–40,42, 45,54, 74, 94, 164
anarchists, 106–108, 123, 128, 133, 136–137, 144
Angiolillo, Michele, 107
Arnold, Samuel, 8, 36
Arthur, Chester, 64, 72, 76, 80, 90, 93, 94
Atzerodt, George, 8, 27, 28, 32, 36, 38, 39

Bay of Pigs invasion, 168–169, 171
Bell, Alexander Graham, 85, 119
Bell, John, 13
Berkman, Alexander, 123
Berlin, Germany, 170, 171, 174
Blaine, James G., 56, 66, 82, 91
Bleeding Kansas, 17–18, 18
Bliss, Willard, 84, 85, 86, 93–94
Booth, John Wilkes, 3–6, 7–8, 8–9, 15, 20, 22, 25, 26–27, 29–31, 33, 36–38, 44, 45
Breckinridge, John C., 13
Bresci, Gaetano, 108
Brown, John, 17, 19–20, 44
Bryan, William Jennings, 113, 116, 117, 124–125
Bull Moose Party, 141–142

rnegie, Andrew, 121–122, 125, 139–140
 not, Sadi, 107
penter, Francis, 15
tillo, Canovas del, 107
se, Salmon, 9
d labor, 104, 120
l rights, 41–42, 50, 54, 94–95, 186
vil War, 3, 7, 8, 9, 11, 13–14, 18, 21–22, 22–23, 23, 44, 50, 52, 72, 74, 95, 96, 111–112, 144
leveland, Grover, 124, 125
old War, 159, 167–168
ommunism, 159, 160, 161, 162, 167, 169, 174, 175, 187, 189
Compromise of 1850, 18

Confederate States of America, 7, 8, 13–14, 20, 21, 22, 43
Conkling, Roscoe, 55, 56, 64, 72–73, 75–76, 80, 91
Connally, John, 178, 181
Cortelyou, George, 130, 132
Cuban Missile Crisis, 172–174
Czolgosz, Leon, 103–106, 107–108, 114, 121, 122, 124, 127, 128–129, 129–130, 130–131, 133, 136–138, 141, 144, 145

Davis, Jefferson, 20
Democratic Party, 125, 142, 178
Douglass, Frederick, 74
Douglas, Stephen, 13

Edison, Thomas, 119
Eisenhower, Dwight, 155, 158, 187, 188
Elisabeth, empress of Austria, 107
Emancipation Proclamation (1863), 22, 36, 44, 74, 96

factories, 70
Ford's Theatre, 25, 27, 29, 33, 45
Forrestal, Mike, 191
Fort Sumter, 20–21
Frick, Henry Clay, 122–123

Garfield, James, 50–52, 57, 59, 64–65, 66, 69, 70–71, 74–75, 76–77, 80, 81–82, 83–84, 85–86, 89, 95, 96, 97
Goldman, Emma, 106–107, 128, 136, 144, 145
Goldwater, Barry, 193
Grant, Ulysses S., 25, 27, 45, 55–56, 72, 73
Guiteau, Charles, 59–62, 64–65, 66–67, 79–81, 81–83, 89, 92–93, 96, 97

Half-Breeds, 73
Hanna, Mark, 125
Harris, Clara, 29
Hayes, Rutherford B., 72, 112
Herold, David, 8, 27, 28, 31, 36, 37, 38
Hobart, Garret, 116
Ho Chi Minh, 187
Homestead Steel Mill, 122–123

Industrial Revolution, 119–121

John Birch Society, 164
Johnson, Andrew, 25, 28, 32, 39–40, 41, 43, 45
Johnson, Lyndon B., 178, 186, 191–193

Kansas-Nebraska Act (1854), 18
Kennedy, John F., 149–155, 159, 167, 168, 169,
    170, 171, 172, 172–173, 175, 177–179,
    185, 186–187, 188, 189, 189–190, 190,
    192, 194, 195
Kennedy, Joseph Jr., 150–151, 154
Kennedy, Joseph, 150–151, 152
Kennedy, Robert, 154
Khrushchev, Nikita, 169, 171, 174, 193

labor strikes, 122–123, 124, 140
Lincoln, Abraham, 3, 4, 6, 8, 9, 11–15, 21, 22,
    23, 25, 27, 29, 30, 33, 35, 38–39, 42, 43,
    44, 45, 55, 74, 81, 84, 96, 97
Lincoln, Mary Todd, 31, 33, 44
Lincoln, Robert Todd, 84
Lister, Joseph, 84–85, 93
Lucheni, Luigi, 107

Mathews, John, 27
McClellan, George B., 23
McKinley, William, 39, 101–103, 108, 111–114,
    114–115, 116–117, 124, 125, 127,
    128–129, 130–131, 131–132, 140,
    141–142, 142–143, 144, 145
McNamara, Robert, 189
Morgan, J.P., 124, 125

New York Customs House, 72, 76
Ngo Dinh Diem, 175, 188–189, 190
Nieman, Fred, 105, 128
Nixon, Richard, 155

O'Laughlen, Michael, 8, 36
Oneida community, 60, 61, 62, 96
Oswald, Lee Harvey, 157–165, 179–181,
    183–186, 194, 195

Panic of 1893, 124, 125
Pendleton Civil Service Act, 90
Pinkerton guards, 123
Pottawatomie Creek Massacre, 17, 19
Powell, Lewis, 8, 27, 28, 31–32, 36, 38

Radical Republicans, 39, 40, 43
Rathbone, Henry, 29, 30
Reconstruction, 23, 39–41, 42, 45
Republican Party, 72, 73, 79, 82, 97, 141
Rockefeller, John D., 121–122, 125, 139–140
Roosevelt, Franklin, 151
Roosevelt, Theodore "Teddy", 39, 115–116, 125,
    133, 135–136, 138–142, 145
Rough Riders, 116
Ruby, Jack, 185, 195

Salvador, Santiago, 107
Santo, Cesare, 107
secession, 6–7, 13, 20, 21, 40
Seward, William, 25, 28, 31–32, 35
Sherman, John, 56
Sherman, William Tecumseh, 82
slavery, 6, 7, 9, 11, 13, 14–15, 17–19, 20, 22, 36,
    40, 97
Spangler, Ned, 36
Spanish-American War, 102, 115–116, 117, 125,
    144
spoils system, 55, 64, 65, 69–70, 71, 72, 89–91,
    94
Stalwarts, 71–72
Stanton, Edwin P., 36, 40, 43, 45
Surratt, John, 8, 9
Surratt, Mary, 8, 26, 36, 38

Taft, Howard, 141, 142
Texas School Book Depository, 165, 179,
    183
Tippit, J.D., 184
Townsend, Smith, 83–84
trusts, 140, 143

Umberto I, king of Italy, 108, 129, 144
USS Maine, 115

Vaillant, Auguste, 107
Vietnam War, 174–175, 186, 187–188, 189–191
    191–193

Walker, Edwin, 164–165
Wilson, Woodrow, 142
World War II, 152–153, 154, 167–168, 194

X-ray machines, 133